SAVOUR

SAVOUR

MARC HIRSCHOWITZ   KAREN ALSFINE   ESTELLE SACHAROWITZ

CONTENTS

Pronounced [kon-tents]

(Noun) The individual items or topics that are dealt with in a publication or document; the *delicious* material, including *recipes and photographs*, in this book.

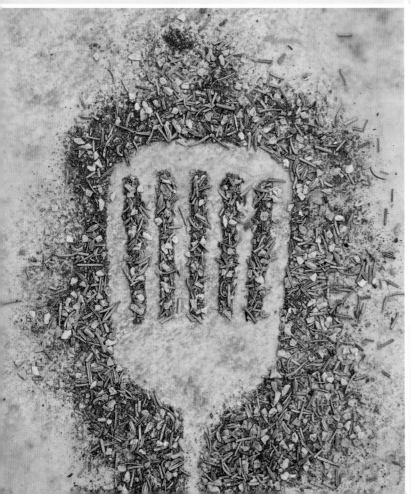

Introduction

Pronounced [in-tr*uh*-duhk-sh*uh*n]

(Noun) Something that introduces as a part of a book or treatise preliminary to the main portion; a little explanation about this book…

There is an innate and indelible bond between food and language. Think about how we describe food: It's … delicious. Yummy. Scrumptious. Heavenly. Aromatic. Flavourful. Wicked. Spicy. Nutty. Crunchy. Fragrant. Icy. Creamy. Chocolaty. Salty. Malty. Delectable. Divine. We often ask: What do you *feel* like eating? The words we use encompass meaning and encapsulate emotion. They instil feeling and facilitate conversation. Sometimes they inspire action. In culinary terms, they resemble a binding agent. They are so much more than their literal form – the letters that create them – much like a delicately prepared dish is so much more than its basic ingredients.

Food speaks to us and we speak about food. Because we are social beings, made to interact and to converse, we often achieve this through food or, more specifically, through eating … together with others, or alone with ourselves.

Words and food – or, how we speak about what we eat – interrelate. In this cookbook, a specific word represents each chapter. The word, its meaning and associated emotions and behaviours, connect with the recipes contained in that chapter. Words are integral. With this book you will be able to eat them … literally. Hopefully, you will savour them too.

When it comes to food, what is it that we savour, *really*? Is it the taste of chocolate, or salt, or lemon? It could be the combination of caramelised onion, or sesame wasabi, or elderflower and mint. Perhaps it's the feeling conjured when we sample such delights, or the conversation we are engaged in at the time. It may be the relationship nurtured over food or the cherished memory a dish evokes. Maybe it's the excursion from the kitchen to the table … or the promise of dessert.

Whether you are a culinary enthusiast, gastronome, adventurous foodie or lover of prepping, kitchen pottering and around-the--table-lingering, **savour** this fondness with *relish*, *appreciation*, *enjoyment* and *utter delight*.

MARC, KAREN AND ESTELLE

Literal
Pronounced [lit-er-*uhl*]
(**Adj.**) Upholding the exact or primary meaning of a word or words; word for word; consisting of, using, or expressed by letters.

Gastronomy
Pronounced [ga-stron-*uh*-mee]
(**Noun**) The art of good eating; the art and practice of choosing, preparing and eating good food.

Literal gastronomy
Pronounced [yum-yum]
(**Verb**) Cooking and eating your words … literally.

WAKEY-WAKEY

Pronounced [weykee weykee]
(Noun) Used for telling someone in a humorous way that they should wake up or should pay attention. **(Verb)** Wake; awaken; get up; waken; rise. **(Verb tr.)** To wake up, and to wake someone up; to break your night's fast; to *ingest energy*; quintessential morning *mood food*; cooking in your pyjamas; the best way to start your day.

Pineapple and mango smoothie

100 ml fresh pulped pineapple
½ cup vanilla yoghurt
juice of 1 lime
1 medium banana, chopped
1 large mango, chopped
1 cup granadilla pulp
2 tsp honey
1 Tbsp chopped almonds (optional)
chopped fresh pineapple, granadilla pulp and a dollop of yoghurt for garnishing

1. Purée all the ingredients in a blender until smooth.
2. Pour into glasses. Garnish with chopped pineapple, granadilla pulp and yoghurt.

Serves 2

Berry smoothie

175 ml frozen yoghurt (vanilla or any berry flavour)
350 g frozen mixed berries
100 ml cranberry juice
1 tsp vanilla essence
castor sugar to taste (optional)
fresh mint leaves for garnishing

1. Process the frozen yoghurt, berries, cranberry juice and vanilla essence in a blender
   until smooth. Adjust tartness to taste by adding a little castor sugar if desired.
2. Pour into glasses and garnish with fresh mint leaves.

Serves 2

Granola

1 Tbsp honey	25 g almonds
1 Tbsp treacle sugar	200 g rolled oats
1 Tbsp maple syrup	15 g pumpkin seeds
1 tsp vanilla essence	15 g sunflower seeds
1 Tbsp butter	30 g shaved coconut
25 g macadamia nuts	

1. Preheat the oven to 160 °C. Grease a baking tray.
2. Heat the honey, treacle sugar, maple syrup, vanilla essence and butter in a saucepan for a few minutes until combined.
3. Place the nuts, oats, seeds and coconut on the tray. Pour over the honey mixture and toss lightly to coat.
4. Bake for 30–40 minutes, shaking the tray and turning the mixture every 10 minutes. Allow to cool and store in a s terilised airtight container.

Serves 4–6

Bircher's muesli

125 g rolled oats
2 cups apple juice
2 unpeeled apples, grated
¼ cup almonds, toasted
a pinch of ground cinnamon

2 Tbsp honey
½ cup thick plain yoghurt
chopped seasonal fresh fruit or chopped dried
mangoes and peaches for serving

1. Soak the oats in the apple juice in the fridge for a few hours or overnight.
2. Combine the grated apple, almonds, cinnamon, honey and yoghurt in a bowl, and fold in the oats.
3. Serve with your choice of fresh or dried fruit.

Serves 4–6

Kippers
with herb butter and creamed leeks

2 whole kippers, butterflied
1 Tbsp unsalted butter
100 g unsalted butter, softened
2 Tbsp Herbamare® organic herb seasoning salt
2 Tbsp olive oil
a bunch of leeks, washed well and thinly sliced
½ cup fresh cream
freshly ground black pepper to taste

1. Wash the kippers and pat dry with paper towels.
2. Heat the 1 Tbsp butter in a frying pan and gently fry the kippers for a few minutes, turning once. Remove from the heat and set aside.
3. In a bowl, mix the softened butter with the seasoning salt. Form the mixture into a small log and wrap in foil. Place in the fridge to set.
4. Heat the olive oil in another frying pan and sauté the leeks for a few minutes. Add the cream and continue to simmer until soft and velvety. Season with black pepper.
5. Place the leeks on a plate, and top with the kippers and dollops of herb butter.

Serves 2

Egg in a basket

1 slice bread per person
a little melted butter
1 egg per person
salt and freshly ground black pepper
a drop of Tabasco® sauce (optional)
smoked salmon strips for garnishing

1. Preheat the oven to 200 °C. Grease a muffin pan very well.
2. Using a rolling pin, flatten the bread and cut off the crusts.
3. Press a slice of bread into a hole in the muffin pan, pushing it into the
   bottom and against the sides. Bake until the bread is slightly brown.
4. Brush the toast cup with a little melted butter and crack an egg into it.
   Return to the oven and bake until the egg is cooked to your preference.
5. Season to taste and add a drop of Tabasco® if desired.
6. If you prefer scrambled egg, cook the egg in a frying pan until almost done,
   then place in the toast cup and finish off in the oven.
7. Garnish with a strip of smoked salmon and serve with roasted rosa tomatoes.

Seeded fruity French toast

6 large eggs
6 Tbsp milk
1 Tbsp castor sugar
a little butter
1 raisin or cranberry and seed or cinnamon loaf, thickly sliced
cinnamon sugar, maple syrup, jam or strawberries and cream for serving

1. Beat the eggs, milk and castor sugar to make a batter.
2. Heat a little butter in a frying pan until hot.
3. Dip the bread slices into the batter, turning them over to soak both sides.
4. Fry the slices in the hot butter until golden, turning to cook both sides. Drain on paper towels.
5. Cut into thick strips and serve immediately with cinnamon sugar, maple syrup, jam or strawberries and cream.

Serves 6

Pancake cake

2 eggs
55 g butter, melted
300 ml milk
1 tsp vanilla essence
300 g cake flour
2 tsp baking powder
4 Tbsp castor sugar
a pinch of salt
¾ cup water

FILLING
340 g mascarpone cheese
340 g crème fraîche
1 tsp vanilla essence
2 Tbsp ground cinnamon
1 cup sugar
5 bananas, sliced and drizzled with fresh lemon juice
3 cups assorted berries (gooseberries, raspberries or blueberries)
1 cup almonds, toasted and roughly chopped
1 cup golden syrup

1. Mix the eggs, melted butter, milk and vanilla essence in bowl.
2. Sift the flour, baking powder, castor sugar and salt into a separate large bowl. Add the butter mixture, whisking continually to form a firm batter. Slowly add the water to create a thinner consistency. Whisk well.
3. Heat a 25 cm non-stick crêpe pan, greased with a little butter. Spoon in the batter to fill the base of the pan. When bubbles appear, turn the pancake over and cook the other side. You should get six large pancakes.
4. To assemble the cake, combine the mascarpone, crème fraîche and vanilla essence by hand.
5. In a separate bowl, mix the cinnamon and sugar.
6. Place one pancake on a serving platter and spread generously with the mascarpone mixture. Scatter over a sixth of the banana slices, berries and almonds, and dust with the cinnamon sugar. Drizzle with syrup and cover with another pancake. Repeat the layers.

Serves 4–6

STORE

Pronounced [stawr, stohr]
(Noun) A stock or supply reserved for future use; a place to keep *culinary* commodities; a warehouse or storehouse, like a *pantry or fridge*, comprising jars of homemade *citrus marmalade* or *poppy seed health rusks*; a great quantity or number; an abundance; plenty; many labelled containers; a domestic stash of stuff you will absolutely need to satisfy an erratic and insatiable craving for *pickled cucumbers*, *marinated olives* or *spiced almonds*. **(Verb tr.)** To put away for expected use; to fill, supply or stock; to save for a rainy day; to delight the DIY, preservative- and colourant-free foodie. Seal your jars, not your lips.

Marinated mushrooms

1 kg mushrooms, washed
1 cup white wine vinegar
1 Tbsp balsamic vinegar
½ cup olive oil
¼ tsp mustard powder
¼ tsp Herbamare® organic
herb seasoning salt
¼ tsp freshly ground
black pepper
¼ cup fresh lemon juice

1. Cook the mushrooms
   in a little water for
   3 minutes. Drain and
   place in a bowl.
2. Mix the rest of the
   ingredients and pour
   over the mushrooms.
3. Marinate overnight
   in the fridge. Store in
   the fridge in a sterilised
   airtight container.

Marinated olives

2 x 200 g pkts Calamata olives, drained
¾ cup olive oil
1 Tbsp crushed garlic
2 tsp chopped fresh parsley
2 tsp chopped fresh origanum
1 tsp coarse ground pepper
1 tsp coarse ground salt
½ cup lemon juice
zest of 1 lemon
2 tsp sugar

1. Combine all the ingredients and place in a sterilised airtight container.
   Marinate for a day and then refrigerate.
2. Serve at room temperature.

Pickled onions

¼ cup sea salt
4 cups water
1 kg pearl onions, peeled
10 fresh red chillies
4 bay leaves
1 Tbsp peppercorns
4 cups white vinegar (for dark onions, use malt vinegar)
¾ cup sugar
1 Tbsp pickling spice

1. Sterilise a large glass jar with a lid in boiling water. (It is better to use lids only once and then discard.)
2. Dissolve the salt in the water in a bowl. Place the onions in the salted water, cover and leave at room temperature overnight.
3. Drain and rinse the onions, and place in the glass jar with the chillies, bay leaves and peppercorns.
4. Over a low heat, cook the vinegar, sugar and pickling spice, stirring continually until the sugar dissolves. Bring to the boil and simmer, uncovered, until the mixture becomes syrupy. Remove from the heat and allow to cool.
5. Strain and pour over the onions.
6. Seal and allow to stand for at least 2 weeks. Refrigerate after opening.

Pickled cucumbers

6 long, thin English cucumbers, cut into thick slices or rounds
6 cups cold water
2 cups vinegar
1 cup sugar
1 Tbsp coarse salt
1 Tbsp peppercorns
4 cloves garlic
1 Tbsp pickling spice

1. Sterilise a large glass jar with a lid in boiling water. (It is better to use lids only once and then discard.)
2. Place the cucumbers in the jar.
3. Boil the remaining ingredients in a saucepan until the sugar dissolves.
4. Pour over the cucumbers. Tightly close the jar and leave out of the fridge for 2–3 days. Then refrigerate.

Pink lemonade cordial

1½ cups sugar
4 cups water
½ cup unsweetened pomegranate juice
½ cup unsweetened grapefruit juice
juice of 4 lemons

1. Place all the ingredients in a large pot and bring to the boil.
    Boil for 8–10 minutes.
2. Remove from the heat, pour into sterilised glass bottles and seal.
    Refrigerate after opening.

Sweet cinnamon plums

12 plums, firm
not bruised
3 cups water
1 cup sugar
¼ cup good red wine
1 cinnamon stick

1. Place the plums in boiling water for about 5 minutes to loosen their skins.
    Drain and peel, then cut in half and remove the pips.
2. Place the water and sugar in a saucepan and boil slowly without stirring.
3. As the mixture thickens, remove from the heat and allow to cool slightly
    before adding the wine and cinnamon stick.
4. Pack the plums tightly into a sterilised jar and ladle over the syrup. Seal and store.

Citrus marmalade

1 medium orange
2 lemons
1 medium grapefruit
2 tsp pectin
6 cups water
1.6 kg warmed sugar (Sugar dissolves more rapidly when it is warm. To warm the sugar,
   place it in a baking dish in the oven at 50 °C for about 20 minutes until it is warm, not hot.)

1. Peel the all fruit and remove the pith and membranes from the peels. Roughly shred the
    peels and set aside. Halve the orange and lemons and squeeze their juices into a large pot.
    Chop the grapefruit flesh into rough chunks and add to the pot.
2. Add the pectin, shredded peels and water.
3. Bring to the boil, then reduce the heat and simmer gently for about 2 hours, until the peels
    become soft and the mixture has reduced by half. Remove from the heat.
4. Add the warmed sugar and stir over a low heat until the sugar has dissolved. Turn the heat to
    high and boil rapidly until a sugar thermometer reads 105 °C.
5. Remove the pot from the heat and skim off any scum from the surface with a slotted spoon.
6. Allow to stand for 15 minutes before pouring into sterilised jars. Leave to set overnight.
    Store in a cool, dark, dry place.

Red onion, cranberry and chilli chutney

3 red onions, coarsely chopped
¼ cup olive oil
2 cloves garlic, chopped
1 tsp chopped fresh red chilli
½ tsp ground ginger
1 tsp salt
2 red apples, peeled, cored and grated
500 g frozen or dried cranberries
¾ cup soft brown sugar
½ cup white wine vinegar
1 cinnamon stick
juice of 1 lemon

1. Sauté the onions in the olive oil over a low heat. Add the garlic, chilli, ginger and salt, and simmer for 5 minutes.
2. Add the apples and cranberries, and simmer for a further 10 minutes.
3. Add the sugar, vinegar, cinnamon stick and lemon juice, and allow to cook over a low heat for 30 minutes, stirring occasionally. Watch that the mixture does not burn.
4. When the chutney has thickened and the liquid has reduced, remove from the heat. Take out the cinnamon stick and pour the chutney into sterilised jars.
5. Store in a cool, dry place for at least 2 weeks before opening. Refrigerate after opening.

Lavender and honey mustard

125 g yellow mustard seeds
125 g black mustard seeds
200 ml cider
3 small shallots, chopped
2 Tbsp honey
1 tsp sea salt
2 Tbsp chopped dried lavender
200 ml white wine vinegar

1. Mix all the ingredients and place in a container with a lid.
2. Allow to stand for 24–36 hours to ferment, then crush the mixture with a mortar and pestle to form a paste.
2. Place in a sterilised jar, seal and store in a cool, dry place. Refrigerate after opening.
4. This has a shelf life of 2 months.

Spiced almonds

2 Tbsp olive oil
2 cups almonds
2 tsp sea salt
1 tsp castor sugar
½ tsp smoked paprika
1 tsp sweet paprika
½ tsp ground cumin
½ tsp cayenne pepper

1. Heat the olive oil in a frying pan and gently cook the almonds for a few minutes until light brown. Drain on paper towels.
2. In a bowl, mix the remaining ingredients. Toss the almonds in the spices to coat and reheat in the pan for 1 minute.
3. Serve warm, or cool and store in an airtight container.

Poppy seed health rusks

1 cup cake flour
7 cups self-raising flour
2 tsp baking powder
2 cups sugar
3 cups All-Bran Flakes®
1 tsp salt
½ cup poppy seeds
2 eggs
2 cups buttermilk
500 g butter

1. Preheat the oven to 180 °C and grease a 30 cm baking tray.
2. Sift the flours and baking powder, and mix with the other dry ingredients in a large bowl. Make a well in the centre.
3. Beat the eggs and buttermilk in a separate bowl.
4. Melt the butter, allow to cool slightly, and then add to the egg mixture.
5. Pour the wet mixture into the dry ingredients and mix well to form a soft dough.
6. Roll the dough into balls and place them next to each other on the baking tray so that they are touching.
7. Bake for 45 minutes until well-risen and golden brown. Remove from the oven, and reduce the heat to 100 °C.
8. Gently break the rusks into pieces or cut through with a knife, and return to the baking tray.
9. Dry in the oven for approximately 4 hours or overnight in a warming drawer.

Makes … a lot

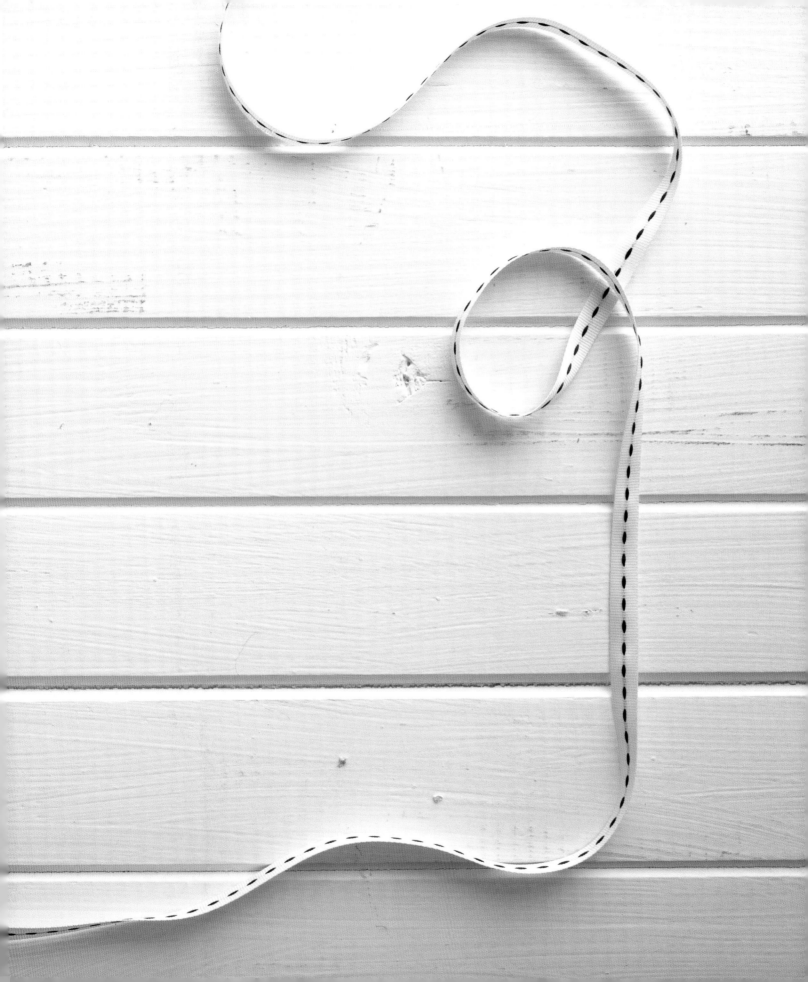

ACCESSORISE

Pronounced [ak-ses-*uh*-riz]
(Verb tr.) To furnish with accessories, trimmings, garnishes and side dishes; to wear or select accessories; to add to; to decorate, supplement, complement, adorn, ornament, augment and embellish; to doll-up; to make prettier, more enticing or irresistibly edible; to scatter with delectable toppings; to drizzle with *sublime sauces*; to coat with love; to add rubs, croutons, coulis, salsas, pesto, and a *foodie-fashionista's must-have* chocolate sauce.

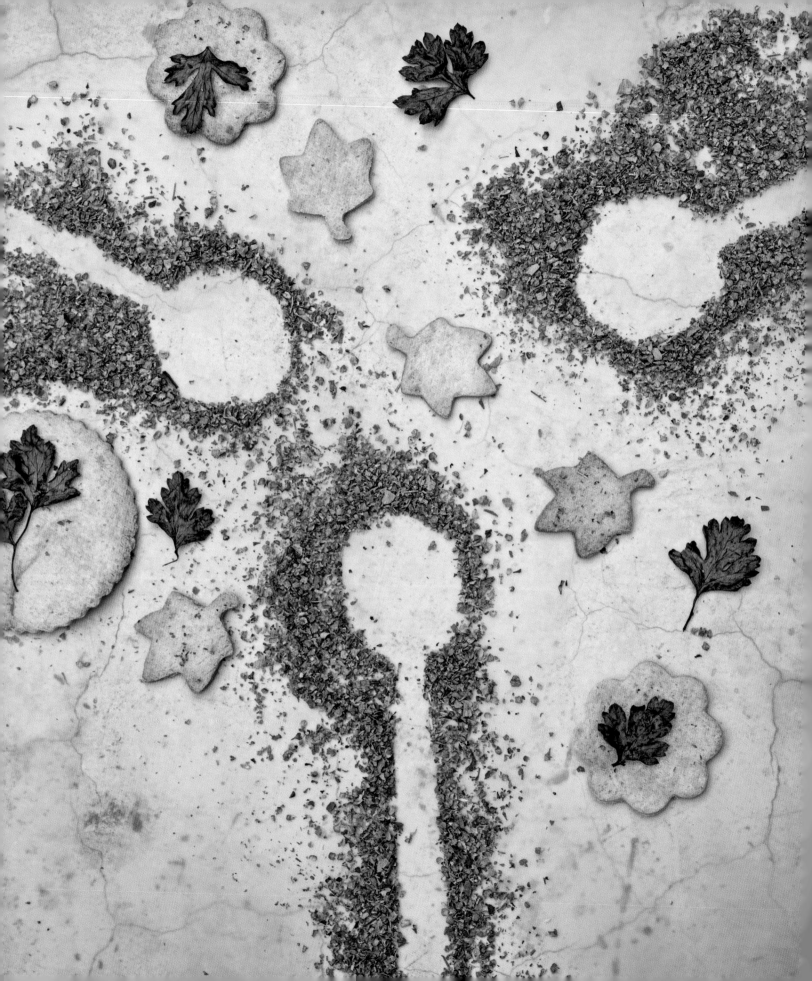

Herbed crouton shapes

white, brown or rye bread, sliced
olive oil
seasoning salt
fresh chervil

1. Preheat the oven to 180 °C.
2. Brush the bread slices with olive oil and lightly sprinkle with seasoned salt.
3. Cut out shapes using cookie cutters – circles, hearts, stars, whatever you prefer.
   Press a piece of fresh chervil into each cutout (for aesthetics).
4. Place the cutouts on a baking tray and bake until golden.
   These will keep in an airtight container for a few days.

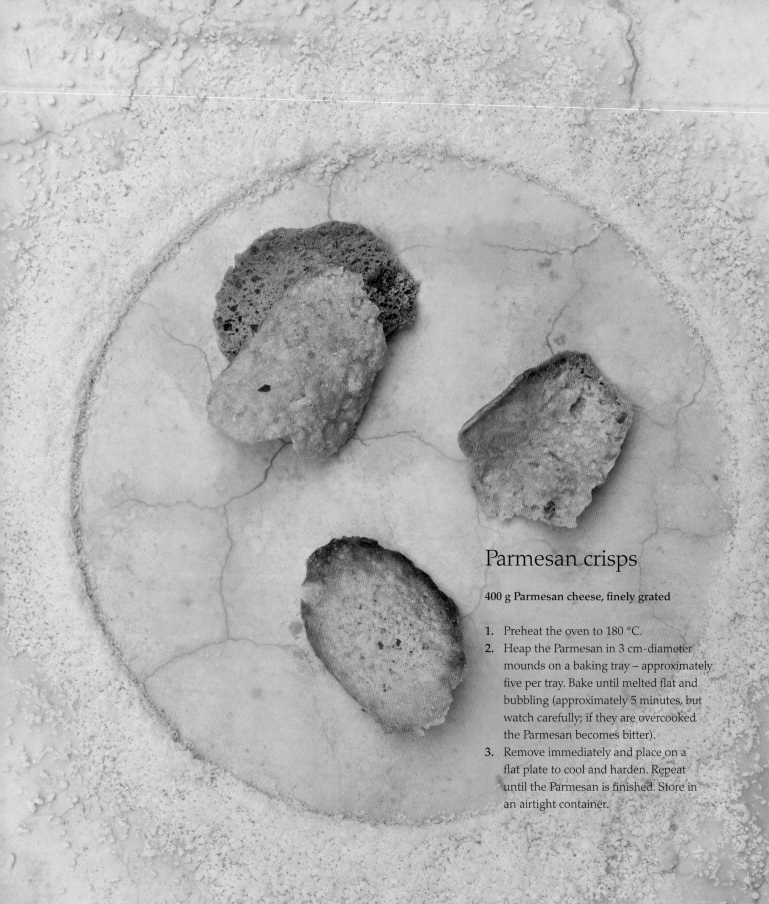

Parmesan crisps

400 g Parmesan cheese, finely grated

1. Preheat the oven to 180 °C.
2. Heap the Parmesan in 3 cm-diameter mounds on a baking tray – approximately five per tray. Bake until melted flat and bubbling (approximately 5 minutes, but watch carefully; if they are overcooked the Parmesan becomes bitter).
3. Remove immediately and place on a flat plate to cool and harden. Repeat until the Parmesan is finished. Store in an airtight container.

Crispy fried capers

1 x 100 g jar capers in brine, drained and dried using paper towels
OR salted capers, soaked in water for 30 minutes, drained and dried
¼ cup olive oil

1. Heat the olive oil in a frying pan. Add the capers, a few at a time
   (be careful of splattering) and cook until brown.
2. Remove and drain on paper towels.

Nori fish rub

1 Tbsp dried origanum
1 Tbsp dried basil
1 tsp dried thyme
2 tsp sea salt
1 tsp dried dill
1 sheet dried nori, chopped

1. Combine all the ingredients
   in a pestle and mortar.
2. Crush to form a powder
   and rub into fish.

Aromatic chicken rub

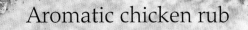

4 tsp dried garlic flakes   2 tsp lemon pepper
4 tsp chopped dried rosemary   1 tsp onion salt
2 tsp cayenne pepper   1 tsp crushed fennel seeds

1. Combine all the ingredients in a small bowl.
2. Rub all over chicken and chill in the fridge
   for a few hours before cooking.

Spicy pineapple salsa

1 pineapple, peeled and chopped
1 Tbsp olive oil
1 Tbsp honey
¼ cup deseeded and chopped yellow pepper
2 Tbsp chopped fresh coriander
¼ cup chopped fresh basil
½ tsp chopped fresh chilli (optional)
2 Tbsp fresh lime juice
¼ tsp Dijon mustard

1. Preheat the oven to 180 °C.
2. Place the pineapple on a baking tray. Toss with the olive oil and honey. Roast for a few minutes until firm.
3. Transfer to a bowl. Combine with the yellow pepper, coriander, basil, chilli, lime juice and mustard.

Serves 4

Tangy fruit salsa

2 firm peaches, peeled, stoned and chopped
3 firm nectarines, peeled, stoned and chopped
1 Tbsp chopped fresh mint
1 tsp castor sugar
1 fresh green chilli, deseeded and chopped
1 Tbsp fresh lime juice

Combine all the ingredients in a bowl.
This makes a wonderful accompaniment to fish.

Serves 4–6

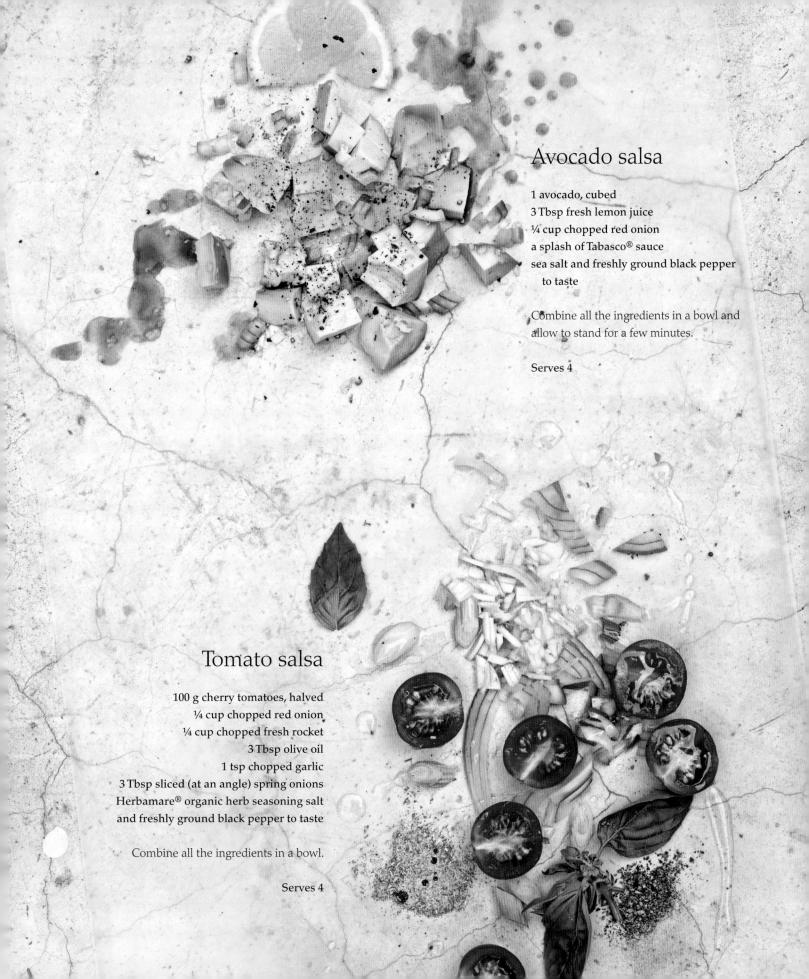

Avocado salsa

1 avocado, cubed
3 Tbsp fresh lemon juice
¼ cup chopped red onion
a splash of Tabasco® sauce
sea salt and freshly ground black pepper
   to taste

Combine all the ingredients in a bowl and
allow to stand for a few minutes.

Serves 4

Tomato salsa

100 g cherry tomatoes, halved
¼ cup chopped red onion
¼ cup chopped fresh rocket
3 Tbsp olive oil
1 tsp chopped garlic
3 Tbsp sliced (at an angle) spring onions
Herbamare® organic herb seasoning salt
and freshly ground black pepper to taste

Combine all the ingredients in a bowl.

Serves 4

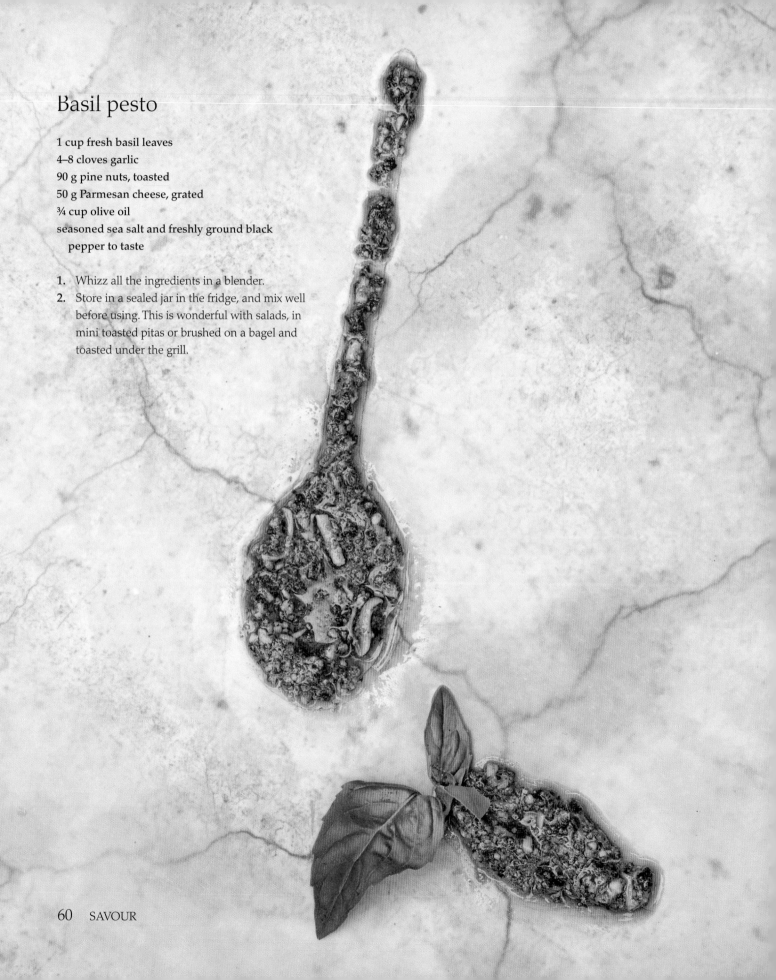

Basil pesto

1 cup fresh basil leaves
4–8 cloves garlic
90 g pine nuts, toasted
50 g Parmesan cheese, grated
¾ cup olive oil
seasoned sea salt and freshly ground black
   pepper to taste

1. Whizz all the ingredients in a blender.
2. Store in a sealed jar in the fridge, and mix well
    before using. This is wonderful with salads, in
    mini toasted pitas or brushed on a bagel and
    toasted under the grill.

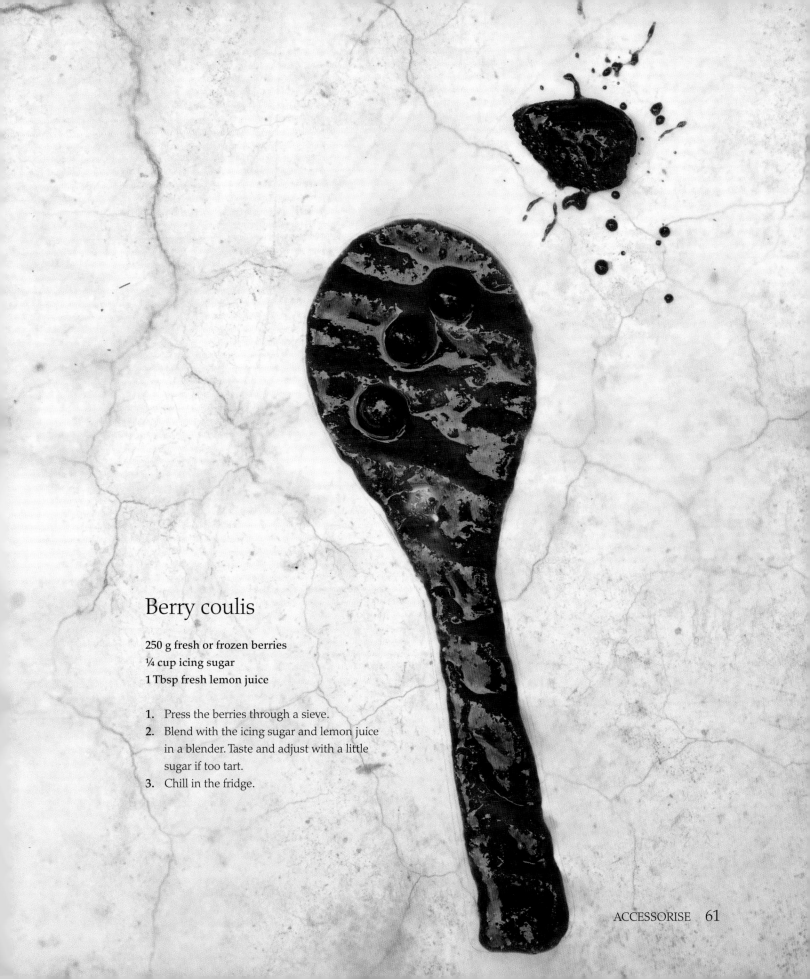

Berry coulis

250 g fresh or frozen berries
¼ cup icing sugar
1 Tbsp fresh lemon juice

1. Press the berries through a sieve.
2. Blend with the icing sugar and lemon juice
   in a blender. Taste and adjust with a little
   sugar if too tart.
3. Chill in the fridge.

Liqueur syrup

200 ml rum
100 g castor sugar
150 g strawberries, hulled and chopped
1 tsp balsamic vinegar

1. Combine the rum, castor sugar,
strawberries and balsamic vinegar in
a saucepan over a medium heat.
2. Simmer uncovered until the liquid
reduces and thickens. This is delectable
drizzled over a berry fruit salad.

Chunky rocky road fudge sauce

200 g good-quality chocolate

25 g butter

1 cup fresh cream

½ tsp vanilla essence

100 g almonds, toasted

100 g glacé cherries

1 cup mini marshmallows

1. In a double boiler, melt the chocolate and butter.
2. Add the cream and vanilla essence. Add the almonds and cherries. Stir until combined.
3. Add the mini marshmallows before serving. Use over ice cream or eat straight off the spoon.

Sweet cinnamon sprinkle

castor sugar and cinnamon (mixed in a 2:1 ratio)
a pinch of ground nutmeg or pimento allspice

Mix the castor sugar and cinnamon with the nutmeg or allspice.
Serve with pancakes or French toast … to add some spice and
satisfy your sweet tooth!

Assorted fresh centred ice cubes

fresh berries or any fruit cut
  into small chunks
fresh mint, whole leaves and
  a few roughly chopped
lemongrass, cut into pieces
edible flowers

1. Fill silicone ice-cube shapes or
   ice trays with water.
2. Place a piece of fruit, a herb or a
   flower in each shape and freeze.
3. Place in jugs when serving
   homemade iced tea, lemon
   water, fruit juices, smoothies,
   cordials or seltzers.

Pronounced [spred]

(Verb tr.) To draw, stretch or open out, especially over a flat surface (like a slice of *zucchini loaf* ... or a delicate white linen tablecloth); to distribute over an area; to dispose in a sheet or coating; to apply *anchovy butter* in a thin (or lusciously thick) layer; to spread *liver pâté on crisp Melba toast*; to overlay or cover *homemade corn bread with a butternut hummus spread*; to smooth creamy *smoked trout pâté* over just-removed-from-the-oven *nutty wheat loaf*. **(Adj.)** Bread and butter at its best. **(Verb)** Break bread and swathe with a spread.

Zucchini loaf

3 eggs
2 cups castor sugar
1½ tsp vanilla essence
1 cup canola oil
3 cups cake flour
¼ tsp baking powder
1 tsp salt
1 tsp bicarbonate of soda
2½ cups grated zucchini (baby marrow)
1¼ cups chopped pecan nuts

1. Preheat the oven to 180 °C. Grease and line two loaf tins with baking paper.
2. Beat the eggs until fluffy. Add the castor sugar, vanilla essence and oil. Beat until the mixture becomes thick.
3. In a separate bowl, sift the flour, baking powder, salt and bicarbonate of soda. Add to the egg mixture and beat.
4. Fold in the marrow and chopped pecans.
5. Pour the batter into the tins and bake for 60–70 minutes.

Makes 2 loaves

Cashew nut butter

250 g cashew nuts

1. Blanch the cashews in boiling water for a few minutes to soften. Remove and dry.
2. Preheat the oven to 180 °C.
3. Place the cashews on a baking tray and toast lightly in the oven. Remove and set ¼ cup aside.
4. Place the remaining cashews in a food processor and whizz until smooth. Scrape this into a bowl.
5. Place the ¼ cup cashews in the food processor and pulse until chopped. Fold the chopped nuts into the smooth cashew butter and serve as a spread for the zucchini loaf above or any bread you fancy.

Corn bread

1 cup cornmeal
1 cup cake flour
2 tsp baking powder
½ tsp bicarbonate of soda
½ tsp salt
1 cup plain yoghurt
1 egg
1 Tbsp honey
3 Tbsp melted butter

1. Preheat the oven to 180 °C. Grease 13 x 6 cm mini loaf tins.
2. Sift together the dry ingredients and stir in the yoghurt, egg, honey and butter.
   Stir until just combined and pour into the tins.
3. Bake for 20 minutes or until a skewer inserted in the centre comes out clean.
   Serve with herb butter.

Makes approximately 6, depending on the size of the tins

Herb butter

100 g unsalted butter, softened
2 Tbsp Herbamare® organic herb seasoning salt

1. In a bowl, mix the softened butter with the seasoning salt.
2. Form the mixture into a small log and wrap in foil. Place in the fridge to set.

Soda bread

250 g white bread flour
250 g brown bread flour
1 tsp salt
2 tsp bicarbonate of soda
55 g butter
2 cups buttermilk

1. Preheat the oven to 200 °C. Grease and flour a baking tray.
2. Combine the dry ingredients in a large bowl and rub in the butter. Make a well in the centre with a wooden spoon and pour in the buttermilk.
3. Stir with a wooden spoon, but as soon as the mixture is well combined, stop stirring – otherwise the dough will become too dense.
4. Place the dough onto a floured board and knead gently into a round shape (approximately 4 cm thick and 18 cm in diameter). Place the dough onto the greased tray. Flatten the top slightly and cut a deep cross into the dough using a sharp floured knife.
5. Bake for 30–40 minutes. The bread is done when it is tapped and sounds hollow.
6. Cool on a wire rack.

Makes 1 loaf

Butternut hummus spread

400 g butternut, cut into chunks
olive oil
sea salt to taste
1 x 430 g tin chickpeas
1 tsp chopped fresh chilli
1 Tbsp fresh lemon juice
1 clove garlic, crushed
1 Tbsp chopped fresh parsley
¼ cup tahini paste

1. Preheat the oven to 180 °C and grease a baking tray.
2. Toss the butternut in olive oil and season with sea salt. Roast on the tray until soft.
3. Place the butternut, chickpeas, chilli, lemon juice, garlic, parsley and tahini paste in a food processor, and blend until smooth. Drizzle with extra olive oil before serving.

Smoked trout pâté

200 g smoked trout, skinned and filleted
½ cup crème fraîche
freshly ground black pepper to taste
1 Tbsp chopped fresh parsley
1 Tbsp creamed horseradish
1 Tbsp spring onion
1 Tbsp fresh lemon juice
½ tsp paprika

1. Blend all the ingredients, keeping the mixture slightly chunky.
2. Adjust seasoning to taste.

Anchovy butter

125 g unsalted butter, softened
2 Tbsp anchovy paste
anchovies, chopped (optional)

1. Place the butter and anchovy paste in a food processor and blend until smooth.
2. Fold in chopped anchovies if desired.
3. Form the mixture into a small log and wrap in foil. Refrigerate until ready to use.
4. Serve with Melba toast or bruschetta or spread into thick slits cut in a baguette and bake in the oven.

Beetroot and mint spread

250 g raw beetroot
olive oil
sea salt to taste
3 Tbsp balsamic vinegar
½ Tbsp fresh lemon juice
½ tsp freshly ground black pepper
1 Tbsp chopped fresh mint
3 Tbsp smooth cream cheese

1. Preheat the oven to 180 °C.
2. Parboil the beetroot for 10 minutes, and then drain.
3. Place the beetroot on a baking tray, brush with olive oil, season
   with sea salt and drizzle over the balsamic vinegar.
4. Roast for 20–30 minutes until soft.
5. Remove and place in a food processor along with the lemon juice,
   black pepper and mint.
6. Blend until smooth, then add the cream cheese and blend again
   until combined.

Chicken liver pâté

2 large onions, sliced
¼ cup olive oil
250 g chicken livers
3 Tbsp chicken or vegetable fat
2 Tbsp sherry or brandy
a pinch of ground cinnamon
1 egg, hard-boiled

1. Sauté the onions in the olive oil in a frying pan until limp.
2. Add the livers and fry until brown (and no blood remains). Allow to cool.
3. Put the livers and onions in a food processor along with the remaining ingredients and liquidise.
4. Taste and adjust seasoning. If the pâté is too thick, add a little hot water to the pan in which you cooked the livers and onions to make a gravy. Add this to the liver pâté.
5. Refrigerate, removing 30 minutes before serving.
6. Serve with pickled cucumbers (see page 32) and lavender and honey mustard (see page 43).

Health loaf

2 cups Nutty Wheat flour   1 Tbsp honey
1 cup cake flour   2 cups plain yoghurt
2 tsp salt   sesame seeds, linseed, sunflower seeds
1½ tsp bicarbonate of soda   for sprinkling

1. Preheat the oven to 180 °C and grease a 28 x 8 cm loaf tin.
2. Mix all the ingredients, except the seeds, in a large bowl.
3. Pour into the tin and sprinkle over the seeds. Bake for 1 hour.

Makes 1 loaf

Fava bean spread

120 g fresh fava (broad) beans (if fresh fava beans are unavailable,
    use boiled fresh green beans or tinned fava beans)
1 x 410 g cannellini beans, drained
½ tsp crushed fresh garlic
1 Tbsp olive oil
1 Tbsp fresh lime juice
1 heaped tsp Herbamare® organic herb seasoning salt
2 tsp chopped fresh sage
sea salt and freshly ground black pepper to taste

1. Boil the fava beans for 5–10 minutes. Drain and carefully peel off the outer membrane.
2. Place all the ingredients in a food processor and blend until smooth. Season to taste.

Pronounced [dee-ahy-wahy]
Do it yourself (abbr DIY): Create something for yourself or perform a task usually done by an expert; construct or assemble something from parts or materials; do everything from scratch; an easy way to feed guests; cooking becomes entertaining; gives an ultimate choice; contains an element of surprise; very cool; works with grown-ups and kids; a *choose-your-own-ending* eating experience; lick your fingers, literally; fun. **Tip:** Be hands-on and supply aprons.

DIY

Olive and caper dip

250 g pitted black olives
250 g pitted green olives
a little crushed garlic
3 Tbsp capers
3 Tbsp anchovies
¼ cup olive oil
freshly ground black pepper to taste

Blitz all the ingredients in a food processor until just mixed and chopped.

Artichoke dip

2 x 400 g tins artichoke hearts
2 Tbsp fresh lemon juice
1 Tbsp mayonnaise
3 Tbsp extra-virgin olive oil
salt and freshly ground black pepper to taste

1. Blitz all the ingredients in a food processor until finely chopped.
2. This is delicious served with cubed avocado.

Feta and piquant pepper dip

250 g feta cheese, cubed
2 Tbsp olive oil
¼ cup juice from the piquant pepper jar
15 piquant peppers, chopped
chilli powder to taste
½ tsp Tabasco® sauce

1. Marinate the feta cubes in the olive oil and piquant pepper juice for 1 hour.
2. Place all the ingredients in a blender and whizz until smooth.

Spicy triangle crisps

1 large laffa bread
½ cup olive oil
1 tsp garlic flakes
1 tsp chilli powder
½ tsp paprika

1. Preheat the oven to 180 °C.
2. Place the laffa on a baking tray and brush with the olive oil. Season with the garlic flakes, chilli powder and paprika. Cut into eight triangles.
3. Bake for 10–15 minutes until brown.

Olive tapenade

500 g pitted Calamata olives
2 cloves garlic, crushed (optional)
3 Tbsp chopped fresh flat-leaf parsley
2 Tbsp fresh lemon juice
¼ cup extra-virgin olive oil
freshly ground black pepper to taste

Blitz all the ingredients in a food processor until finely chopped or smooth.

Cream cheese and pecan dip

250 g cream cheese
½ tsp garlic flakes
1 Tbsp chopped fresh parsley
½ tsp chopped fresh chives
2 Tbsp sour cream
100 g pecans, lightly toasted and roughly chopped

Combine all the ingredients, except the pecans, in a serving bowl. Top with the pecans.

Herbed garlic bread

1 baguette
⅔ cup olive oil
finely grated rind of 1 lemon
4 cloves garlic, crushed
1½ Tbsp chopped fresh chives
¼ cup chopped fresh flat-leaf parsley
¼ cup chopped fresh dill

1. Preheat the oven to 200 °C.
2. Cut the bread into 1.5 cm-thick slices – do not cut all the way through.
3. In a bowl, mix the olive oil, lemon rind, garlic, chives, parsley and dill.
4. Brush both sides of each slice of bread with the garlic-herb mixture and wrap the bread tightly in foil.
5. Place on a baking tray and bake for 20–25 minutes.
6. Slice through and serve warm.

Serves 6–8

Hummus dip

250 g ready-made hummus
1 Tbsp fresh lemon juice
1 Tbsp olive oil
1 avocado, chopped (optional)
a little extra fresh lemon juice
freshly ground black pepper to taste
1 cup chickpeas
1 red pepper, deseeded and chopped
a little olive oil
paprika to taste

1. Mix the hummus, lemon juice and olive oil, and place in a serving bowl.
2. Sprinkle the chopped avocado (if using) with a little lemon juice and season with black pepper. Toss with the hummus.
3. Garnish with the chickpeas and red pepper.
4. Drizzle with olive oil and season with paprika and black pepper.

Greek tzatziki

1 English cucumber, chopped
2 cloves garlic, crushed
200 ml plain yoghurt
1 Tbsp olive oil
1 Tbsp chopped fresh mint

1. Place the cucumber in a food processor and whizz.
2. Add the remaining ingredients and blend until combined.

Crispy long Italian bread

1 long Italian baguette
olive oil
garlic
salt and freshly ground black pepper

1. Preheat the oven to 180 °C.
2. Cut the bread lengthways and rub with olive oil, garlic, salt and pepper.
3. Place on a baking tray and grill until golden and crispy. Serve with a variety of toppings.

Sautéed sweet red pepper, anchovy and olive pasta sauce

¾ cup olive oil
½ tsp crushed garlic (optional)
2 red onions, coarsely chopped
2 large red peppers, deseeded and coarsely chopped
freshly ground black pepper to taste
12 good-quality anchovies, cut lengthways (check for bones)
25 large pitted Calamata olives (optional)
240 g mozzarella cheese, cubed
fresh flat-leaf parsley for garnishing

1. Heat ½ cup of the olive oil in a saucepan.
2. Add the garlic (if using) and onions, and fry for a few minutes.
3. Add the red peppers and sauté until al dente.
4. Remove from the heat.
5. Add the remaining olive oil to coat the mixture and season with black pepper.
6. Add the anchovies and olives (if using), and mix.
7. Reheat, pour into a serving bowl, top with the mozzarella cubes and garnish with parsley.
8. To dress it up, you can add a few extra anchovies and olives before serving. Serve with cooked pasta.

Serves 4–6

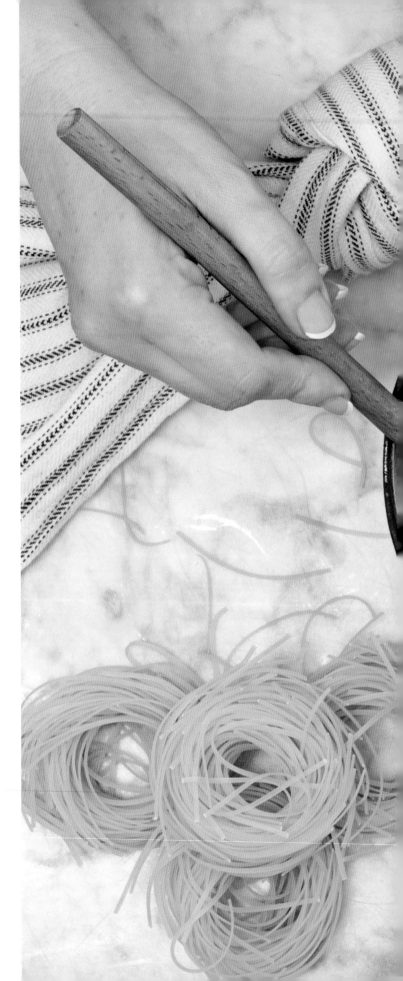

Asparagus, broccoli and pea medley pasta sauce

¾ cup olive oil
½ tsp crushed garlic
2 onions, coarsely chopped
250 g long-stemmed broccoli, coarsely chopped
240 g green asparagus, cut into thirds
240 g shelled garden peas
2 x 400 g tins artichoke hearts, coarsely chopped
½ cup pesto
1 tsp deseeded and chopped fresh green chilli
coarse salt and freshly ground black pepper to taste
1 cup pine nuts, toasted

1. Heat ½ cup of the olive oil in a saucepan and fry the garlic and onions until limp.
2. Add the broccoli, asparagus and peas, and sauté until al dente.
3. Add the artichokes, pesto, chilli and an extra 3 Tbsp olive oil.
4. Season with salt and pepper to taste.
5. Remove the pan from the heat and toss the vegetables with the remaining olive oil.
6. Sprinkle over the toasted pine nuts just before serving with cooked pasta.

Serves 4–6

Slow-roasted rustic Italian tomato pasta sauce

This recipe has two parts, but they're easy and worth the effort.

PART 1: RUSTIC SLOW-ROASTED TOMATOES

8 roma or ripe Italian tomatoes, quartered

olive oil for drizzling

1 clove garlic, roughly chopped

garlic pepper to taste

1. Preheat the oven to 180 °C.
2. Place the tomatoes on a baking tray. Drizzle with olive oil, sprinkle over the chopped garlic and season with garlic pepper.
3. Roast until tender, approximately 30 minutes.
4. Discard the garlic before serving.

PART 2: SMOOTH NAPOLETANA SAUCE

3 Tbsp olive oil

2 medium onions, chopped

3 medium carrots, peeled and grated

3 x 400 g tins Italian tomatoes

garlic pepper and coarse salt to taste

a handful of chopped fresh basil

1. Heat the olive oil in a saucepan over a high heat and sauté the onions.
2. Add the carrots and sauté for a few more minutes.
3. Add the tomatoes, lower the heat and boil, uncovered, until the sauce reduces and thickens (this can take an hour depending on how watery the tomatoes are – but watch carefully to make sure the sauce doesn't stick to the pan).
4. Season with garlic pepper and coarse salt.
5. Blend the sauce in a blender, keeping it slightly coarse.
6. Before serving, fold in the slow-roasted tomatoes and sprinkle with the chopped basil.
7. Serve with cooked pasta.

Serves 4–6

Creamed four-cheese pasta sauce

30 g butter
400 ml fresh cream
150 g Gorgonzola cheese, crumbled
150 g Gruyère cheese, grated
150 g pecorino cheese, grated
250 g Parmesan cheese, grated
freshly ground black pepper to taste
fresh flat-leaf parsley for garnishing

1. Melt the butter in a saucepan, add the cream, lower the heat and simmer for a few minutes. The butter-cream mixture will thicken slightly and reduce.
2. Remove from the heat and slowly add the four cheeses, stirring until smooth and deliciously, creamily cheesy.
3. Whizz the sauce with a stick blender and season with some black pepper.
4. Return to the pan and gently reheat, without boiling.
5. Serve with cooked pasta and garnished with parsley.
6. Have a wedge of Parmesan cheese and a small grater on hand.

Serves 4–6

Marinated linefish envelopes

500 g firm white linefish or salmon, filleted, deboned and cut into 4 cm cubes
¼ cup soy sauce
2 Tbsp teriyaki sauce
1½ Tbsp honey
2 Tbsp mirin
1 Tbsp olive oil
1 clove garlic, thinly sliced
6 pieces nori
3 cups sushi rice, prepared according to the packet instructions
1 cup sesame seeds, toasted

1. Place the fish in a large flat-bottomed bowl, and add the soy sauce, teriyaki sauce, honey and mirin.
2. Baste and marinate the fish for 45 minutes (if you leave it longer the fish may become too salty).
3. In a saucepan, heat the olive oil and gently fry the garlic.
4. Add the fish (without the marinade) and cook for approximately 10 minutes, turning continuously, until slightly crisp.
5. Fold each piece of nori in half, tear along the fold, fold again and tear, making squares.
6. To assemble, place a spoon of sushi rice on the nori, followed by a piece of fish and a sprinkling of toasted sesame seeds.
7. Fold, making an envelope, and pop in your mouth.
8. Alternatively, secure with a toothpick or wooden skewer.

Serves 4–6

Deconstructed meringue, phyllo cups and zesty passion fruit curd

PASSION FRUIT CURD
3 large eggs, at room temperature
¾ cup white sugar
⅓ cup granadilla juice
125 g butter, at room temperature
1½ Tbsp granadilla pulp
1 Tbsp fresh lemon juice

PHYLLO CUPS
1 x 500 g box phyllo pastry
125 g butter, melted
icing sugar for dusting

MERINGUES
1 cup egg whites
a pinch of salt
2 cups sifted white sugar
2 tsp vanilla essence
2 tsp vinegar

1. First make the passion fruit curd. Whisk the eggs, sugar and granadilla juice in a double boiler. Stir continuously to prevent the mixture from curdling. When it becomes thick, remove from the heat. If there are lumps, strain the mixture. Add the butter, granadilla pulp and lemon juice and whisk until smooth. Cover the bowl with a damp cloth and allow to cool, then refrigerate. The mixture will keep for a week.
2. Next make the phyllo cups. Preheat the oven to 180 °C. Spray a mini-muffin pan with non-stick cooking spray. Cut the phyllo sheets into 8 cm squares. Brush each with melted butter. Arrange five squares on top of each other, placing each square in a different direction. (This will create an interesting jagged edge once baked.) Press each stack into a hole in the mini-muffin pan. Bake for 10–12 minutes until golden brown. Allow to cool before removing from the pan. Arrange on a large flat tray and dust with icing sugar.
3. To make the meringues, allow the oven to again reach 180 °C. Line a baking tray with baking paper. Using an electric beater, whisk the egg whites and salt for 1 minute. Beat for a further 2 minutes on medium speed and then on high speed until white and frothy. While beating, slowly add the sugar a little at a time. Add the vanilla essence and vinegar and beat for another 1 minute. Pipe the meringue mixture in small blobs onto the lined baking tray. Turn down the oven to 110 °C and bake the meringues for 1½ hours. Turn off the oven and leave the meringues inside until cool.
4. Serve the phyllo cups, meringues and passion fruit curd separately so that guests can construct their own lemon meringue pies.

Makes 36

Warm milk, chocolate swirls and crushed cookies

200 g Toblerone® chocolate
4 x 50 g Mars® bar chocolates or Bar-One® chocolates
¾ cup fresh cream
1 x 175 g box Oreo® biscuits, crushed
1 x 100 g box any chocolate-coated honeycomb biscuits
4 cups milk, warmed

1. Melt the Toblerone® and Mars® bars or Bar-Ones®
   in a double boiler.
2. Stir in the cream until blended and heated through.
3. Use a toothpick dipped in the chocolate sauce
   to draw swirls on the inside of four tall glasses.
4. On a large tray, arrange a bowl filled with crushed
   Oreo® and honeycomb biscuits, carafes of warm milk,
   a jug of the hot chocolate sauce, the glasses and some
   long spoons.

Serves 4

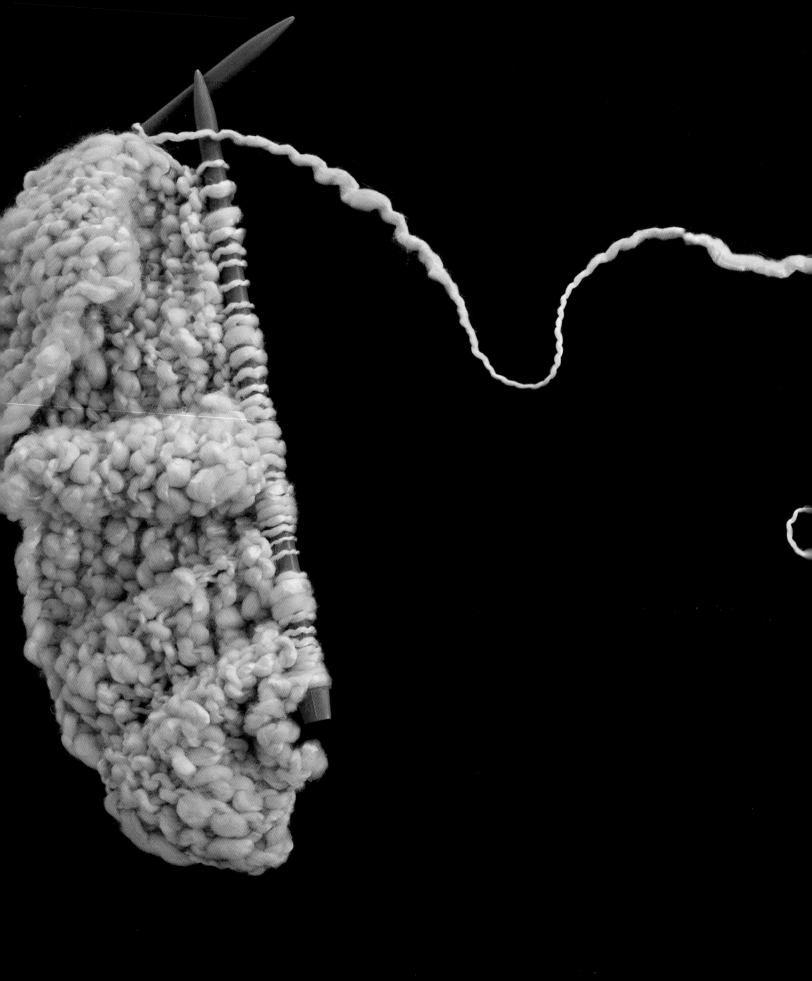

Pronounced [slurp]
(Verb tr.) To ingest (food or drink) with a sucking noise; to make loud sounds while eating or drinking; to slurp a mouthful; to slosh around the bowl; to wallow in warmth; to *dunk bread* into; to top with a *dithering dollop of cream*; to soak up the flavour; to ingest *warm liquid* with gusto, allowing it to infuse chilled bones. **(Noun)** An intake of food or drink with a somewhat raucous sucking swish; a lapping or splashing reverberation, sometimes created without a spoon-like utensil but by simply lifting the bowl to one's lips and ... well, sluuuuuurping. **Caution:** May be hazardous to neckties.

Artichoke cream soup

2 x 400 g tins artichoke hearts
3 Tbsp butter
2 cups milk, gently heated
2 medium potatoes, peeled, boiled and mashed
2 cups vegetable stock
salt and freshly ground black pepper to taste
fresh cream and olive oil for serving

1. Drain the artichokes, keeping the liquid. Slice and sauté the artichokes in 2 Tbsp of the butter in a pot until soft.
2. Add the reserved liquid and hot milk, and cook gently for about 15 minutes.
3. Add the mashed potatoes and stock, and stir well.
4. Blend the soup in a food processor, strain and season to taste.
5. Return to the pot and reheat before adding the remaining 1 Tbsp butter. Serve with a drizzle of cream and olive oil.

Serves 4–6

French onion soup
with cheese croutons

50 g butter
1 kg onions, thinly sliced
1 tsp salt
1 Tbsp cake flour
3 litres beef or vegetable stock
salt and freshly ground black pepper to taste
¼ cup port

1. Melt the butter in a large pot. Stir in the onions and salt and cook, uncovered, for approximately 20 minutes until the onions are golden brown. Stir occasionally.
2. Remove from the stove and sprinkle over the flour. Return to the heat and stir continuously for 2–3 minutes. Remove from the heat and set aside.
3. In a separate pot, heat the stock. Add the stock to the onions, return to a low heat and simmer, partially covered, for 30–40 minutes. Skim off the fat occasionally. Season to taste, add the port and simmer for a further 10 minutes.
4. Serve with the cheese croutons below.

CHEESE CROUTONS
12–16 x 2 cm-thick slices French bread
olive oil for brushing
1 clove garlic, sliced
grated Gruyère, sliced goat's cheese rounds or grated Cheddar, enough to cover the bread

1. Preheat the oven to 180 °C.
2. Place the bread on a baking tray and brush with a little olive oil. Scatter over the garlic and top with the cheese.
3. Bake for 15 minutes, then turn over the slices and bake for a further 5 minutes.
4. Float the cheese croutons on top of the individual servings of soup.

Serves 4–6

Pumpkin and honey soup

2 cloves garlic, chopped
2 leeks, chopped
a little olive oil
3 litres water
2 kg pumpkin, peeled and cut into chunks
3 heaped Tbsp chicken stock powder
3 Tbsp honey
4 tsp sea salt
4 tsp freshly ground black pepper
chilli powder to taste
½ cup thick plain yoghurt
toasted chopped cashews for serving
pumpkin seeds for serving

1. Sauté the garlic and leeks in a little olive oil in a large pot.
2. Add the water, pumpkin, stock powder and honey. Boil for approximately 40 minutes until the pumpkin is tender.
3. Whizz the soup in a blender, add the salt and pepper, and adjust the taste with chilli powder.
4. If too thick, you can add a little extra water.
5. Fold in the yoghurt and serve with a sprinkling of chopped cashews and pumpkin seeds.

Serves 4–6

Chicken soup

olive oil for frying
6 leeks, finely chopped
1 small onion, chopped
8 medium carrots, peeled and grated
6 baby marrows, grated
1 medium butternut, peeled and grated
8 litres water
1 whole chicken, well cleaned
500 g giblets
1 bay leaf
3 potatoes, peeled and grated
3 Tbsp chicken stock powder
freshly ground black pepper to taste

1. Heat a little olive oil in a pot and fry the leeks and onion until soft.
2. Add the carrots, marrows, butternut and water, and bring to the boil.
3. Add the chicken, giblets, bay leaf and potatoes.
4. Reduce the heat to medium and skim the fat from the surface. Add the stock powder.
5. Simmer for 45 minutes, then boil for approximately 25 minutes until the chicken and potatoes are cooked.
6. Season with black pepper and a little more stock powder if needed.
7. Cool slightly before removing the chicken and giblets. You can either serve the soup with the chicken (skin removed, deboned and chopped) and giblets, or strain and serve as a clear soup.

Serves 6–8

Coconut and mushroom soup

a little olive oil

1 kg button mushrooms, thickly sliced (before slicing, wipe the mushrooms gently with damp paper
   towels – do not wash them as they will become watery)

1 shallot, chopped

1 small red onion, chopped

1 Tbsp chopped garlic

1 fresh chilli, deseeded and chopped

3 Tbsp crushed fresh ginger

1 x 410 g tin coconut cream

3 cups water

2 stalks lemongrass, chopped

1 Tbsp chicken stock powder

1 Tbsp chopped fresh coriander

1 tsp powdered galangal

1 heaped Tbsp desiccated coconut

salt and freshly ground black pepper to taste

90 g soba noodles

chopped spring onions for serving (optional)

1. Heat the oil in a saucepan and lightly fry the mushrooms. Remove and set aside.
2. Add a little more oil to the same pan and sauté the shallot, red onion, garlic, chilli and ginger
   for a few minutes.
3. Over a medium heat, add the coconut cream, water, lemongrass, stock powder, coriander,
   galangal and coconut.
4. Boil for 20 minutes until the mixture reduces and thickens slightly. Season with salt and
   black pepper.
5. Whizz the soup in a blender, then return to the saucepan.
6. Add the mushrooms and boil for a further 30 minutes.
7. In the meantime, cook the noodles according to the packet instructions.
8. When ready to serve, add the noodles to the soup and adjust the seasoning. Top with spring
   onions if desired.

Serves 4–6

Salmon bisque

a little olive oil
200 g fresh mushrooms, sliced
1 large onion, chopped
1 tsp minced garlic
2 Tbsp cornflour
2 cups milk
2 vegetable stock cubes, crumbled
1 x 415 g tin salmon, deboned and flaked
1 x 400 g tin cream of tomato soup
1 tsp sugar
½ tsp Worcestershire sauce
8 spring onions, finely chopped
2 tsp finely chopped fresh chilli
2 Tbsp sherry
fresh cream for serving
chopped fresh parsley, chives or spring onion for garnishing
freshly ground red peppercorns for garnishing

1. Heat a little olive oil in a pot and sauté the mushrooms, onion and garlic until limp.
2. Stir in the cornflour and slowly add the milk. Stir in the crumbled stock cubes.
3. Add the salmon and stir to mix. Add the tomato soup, sugar, Worcestershire sauce, spring onions and capsicum.
4. Stir in the sherry and simmer for 15–20 minutes until the soup thickens.
5. If the consistency is too thick, add a little more water or milk. If you prefer a smoother bisque, whizz in a blender.
6. Serve garnished with a dollop of cream and a sprinkling of chopped parsley, chives or spring onion and freshly ground red peppercorns.

Serves 4–6

CHILL

Pronounced [chil]
(Noun) A sensation of coldness. **(Adj.)** Moderately cold; chilly. **(Verb tr.)** To lower in temperature; to cool; to calm down; to relax; to refrigerate; to serve iced; to infuse with coolness on a long, hot, lazy afternoon; to *chill out*; to keep company; to melt in your mouth.

Smooth avocado soup

2 small avocados or 1 large, chopped
½ cup fresh lemon juice
1 Tbsp chopped red onion
2½ cups milk
1 tsp Tabasco® sauce
½ cup sour cream
salt and freshly ground black pepper to taste
chopped fresh chives and cucumber ribbons for garnishing

1. Whizz the avocados, lemon juice, red onion and 1 cup of the milk in a blender.
2. Add the Tabasco® sauce, sour cream and more milk until you create the desired consistency. The soup should not be too thin and milky. Season to taste.
3. Chill the soup before serving in chilled bowls.
4. Garnish with chopped chives and cucumber ribbons.

Serves 4–6

Cool pea soup

2 Tbsp olive oil
1 onion, chopped
3 leeks, chopped
1 clove garlic, chopped
1.5 litres boiling water
2 Tbsp beef, chicken or vegetable
  stock powder
1 kg frozen petits pois
salt and freshly ground black pepper
  to taste
1½ cups plain yoghurt
fresh mint and micro leaves for serving

1. Heat the oil in a pot and fry the
   onion, leeks and garlic until soft.
2. Add the boiling water and
   stock powder.
3. Add the petits pois and boil for
   approximately 10 minutes.
4. Remove from the heat and allow to
   cool before blending until smooth.
5. Season with salt and pepper.
6. Stir in the yoghurt and top with the
   mint and micro leaves before serving.

Serves 4–6

Chilled beetroot soup
with baby potatoes and
sour cream

1 kg fresh beetroot, well cleaned
   (do not peel)
3 litres water
1 tsp tartaric acid
2 tsp sugar
juice of 1 lemon
1 Tbsp salt
freshly ground black pepper to taste
boiled baby potatoes and sour cream
   for serving

1. Boil the beetroot in the water until
   tender. Allow to cool. Do not drain.
2. Coarsely grate five beetroot
   and set aside.
3. Blend the remaining beetroot
   with 2 litres of the boiled water
   used to cook the beetroot.
4. Add the grated beetroot, tartaric acid,
   sugar, lemon juice and salt. Adjust
   seasoning to taste. Refrigerate.
5. Serve with boiled baby potatoes and
   sour cream.

Serves 8–10

Beetroot carpaccio
with watermelon and goat's cheese

12 fresh beetroot
olive oil for brushing
vegetable seasoning for sprinkling
½ watermelon
¼ cup chopped fresh mint
1½ cups crumbled goat's cheese
½ cup lightly roasted and roughly chopped pistachios

DRESSING
2 Tbsp white wine vinegar
6 Tbsp olive oil
2 tsp honey
1 clove garlic, chopped
sea salt and freshly ground black pepper to taste

1. Parboil the beetroot for about 30 minutes, depending on their size. Remove the beetroot, allow to cool, and then peel and slice into very thin rounds.
2. Preheat the oven to 180 °C. Grease a baking tray.
3. Place the beetroot rounds on the baking tray, brush with olive oil and sprinkle with vegetable seasoning. Roast in the oven for 30 minutes until soft and lightly browned.
4. In the meantime, make the dressing. Simply whizz all the ingredients in a blender and pour into a small jug.
5. When cooked, allow the beetroot to cool, and then place on a platter, overlapping and piling the slices slightly.
6. Scoop the watermelon into balls and scatter over the beetroot. Sprinkle with the mint, goat's cheese and pistachios, and drizzle over the dressing.
7. Alternatively, slice the watermelon and goat's cheese into rounds and create stacks as shown opposite.

Serves 6

Gravadlax

1 side fresh salmon, approximately 1 kg, skin on but filleted
¼ cup sea salt
¼ cup ground peppercorns
3 Tbsp castor sugar
1 cup chopped fresh dill
2 Tbsp vodka, gin, rum or whiskey (optional)
a few sprigs of fresh dill

1. Line a rectangular ceramic dish with clingfilm.
2. Wash and pat dry the salmon. Place the side of salmon in the dish, skin-side down.
3. Mix the salt, peppercorns and castor sugar, and sprinkle on top of the salmon, pressing it into the flesh.
4. Sprinkle over the chopped dill and rub well.
5. Brush the fish with the liquor, if using. Place a few sprigs of dill on top.
6. Wrap the salmon tightly in the clingfilm. Cover the dish with a tray and weigh down with weights (tins or small bricks work).
7. Refrigerate for 2–3 days. Check every 24 hours, pouring off any liquid and turning the fish over.
8. Before serving, scrape off the dill, salt and peppercorns. Slice and serve with fresh bread and a herb or mustard sauce. Alternatively, slice and add to salads.

Serves 8–10

Refreshing citrus granita

4 cups cold water
1 cup castor sugar
4 cups fresh pineapple pulp (crush pineapple in a blender)
½ cup fresh orange juice
a pinch of salt
orange rind for garnishing

1. Heat the water and sugar in a saucepan over
    a low heat, stirring until the sugar dissolves.
2. Add the pulp, juice and salt, and stir for a
    few minutes. Remove from the heat and cool.
3. Pour the mixture into a shallow metal dish and
    freeze. When the mixture begins to set, use a fork
    to break up the ice.
4. Freeze and repeat every few hours until the mixture
    has completely set.
5. Spoon into chilled bowls and serve garnished with strips
    of orange rind.

Serves 6

Very merry berry mint sorbet

250 g castor sugar
200 ml water
30 g fresh mint, chopped
700 g mixed berries
juice of 1 lemon

1. Heat the castor sugar and water in a saucepan over a low heat, stirring until the sugar dissolves. Remove from the heat, add the mint and allow to stand for 10 minutes.
2. In a separate pot, slowly cook the berries and lemon juice for a few minutes until softened. Remove from the heat.
3. Whizz the berries and sugar mixture together in a blender. Strain through a sieve to remove the seeds.
4. Either churn the mixture in an ice-cream maker according to the instructions or place in a shallow container and freeze, stirring every few hours to break up the ice crystals. You can even place the sorbet in a blender for a quick whizz until smooth, then return to the freezer.
5. Serve with fresh berries and fresh mint.

Serves 4–6

Languid liquorice ice cream

200 g soft black liquorice
1 cup water
2 litres good-quality vanilla
ice cream, softened
chopped liquorice or liquorice allsorts

1. Place the liquorice and water
    in a double boiler.
2. Melt until soft, but not too
    smooth. There should be a few
    liquorice lumps.
3. Fold the mixture into the softened
    ice cream.
4. Transfer to a serving bowl or a lined
    1-litre (300 x 105 x 70 mm) baking
    tin and freeze.
5. Serve in scoops topped with hopped
    liquorice or liquorice allsorts.

Serves 6–8

Soothing green tea-infused vanilla ice cream

1 cup fresh cream
1 x 385 g tin condensed milk
4 eggs, separated
2 tsp vanilla essence
5 green tea tea bags

1. Beat the cream until thick and fluffy.
2. In a separate bowl, beat the condensed milk and egg yolks. Add the vanilla essence and fold in the cream.
3. Beat the egg whites in a separate bowl and fold into the mixture.
4. Remove the tea leaves from four of the tea bags and, with a pestle and mortar, crush the leaves to a fine powder. Fold this into the mixture.
5. Transfer to a ceramic dish or any suitable freezer-friendly container and freeze.
6. When ready to serve, make a cup of green tea in tepid water with the remaining tea bag.
7. Scoop the ice cream into dessert bowls and pour over the tea just before serving.

Serves 6–8

PURE

Pronounced [py*oor*]

(Adj.) Having a homogeneous or uniform composition; not mixed; free from impurities; containing nothing inappropriate or extraneous; complete; wholesome nutrition; combining nature's *best ingredients*; from the farmer's market or garden; maximum nutritional benefit; containing nothing that does not properly belong; pure bliss; food resembling its glorious self.

All-green salad with herb dressing

If you want to make this into a main summer salad meal, add tuna, smoked salmon, cottage cheese or leftover sliced fillet.

1 large pkt mixed lettuce
1 small pkt Belgian endive
40 g fresh herbs
120 g edamame
120 g sugar snap peas
100 g asparagus tips, stems cut at an angle
beetroot sprouts or other sprouts for garnishing

OPTIONAL ADDITIONS
rocket, peas, fennel, chicory, avocado, cucumber, palm hearts, artichoke hearts

DRESSING
¾ cup olive oil
¼ cup white wine vinegar
1 clove garlic, finely chopped
1 Tbsp finely chopped fresh parsley
1 Tbsp chopped chives
1 Tbsp Dijon mustard
2 tsp brown sugar
sea salt and freshly ground black pepper to taste

1. Toss the salad ingredients in a bowl and garnish with sprouts.
2. Using a stick blender, whisk the dressing ingredients and drizzle over the salad.

Serves 4–6

Roquefort salad

with French loaf croutons and creamy dressing

Make the dressing the day before.

DRESSING

1 spring onion, chopped

1 cup mayonnaise

1 clove garlic, crushed

¼ cup chopped fresh parsley

½ cup fresh cream

¼ cup white vinegar

1 Tbsp fresh lemon juice

¾ cup crumbled Roquefort cheese

¼ tsp sea salt

¼ tsp freshly ground black pepper

CROUTONS

1 French loaf, sliced very thin at an angle

olive oil for brushing

sea salt and mixed dried herbs to taste

SALAD

2 pkts cos lettuce

400 g cherry tomatoes

10 mini Israeli cucumbers, sliced

12 pitted black olives

1 x 410 g tin artichoke hearts, quartered

150 g mushrooms, sliced

1 yellow pepper, deseeded and thinly sliced

1 red pepper, deseeded and thinly sliced

6 spring onions, chopped

½ cup crumbled Roquefort for garnishing

1. To make the dressing, mix the spring onion, mayonnaise, garlic and parsley. Stir in the cream. Add the vinegar, lemon juice and Roquefort. Beat well and season with the salt and pepper. Chill overnight to blend the flavours.
2. To make the croutons, preheat the oven to 180 °C. Brush the French loaf slices with olive oil and season with sea salt and herbs. Place on a baking tray and bake until the bread looks like toast.
3. Arrange the salad ingredients in a bowl or on a platter. Drizzle with the dressing, sprinkle over some extra crumbled Roquefort and top with the croutons.

Serves 4–6

Marinated barbecued chicken salad

6 chicken breast fillets
1 Tbsp chicken spice
2 tsp seasoned sea salt
3 Tbsp honey
juice and zest of 2 lemons
3 Tbsp olive oil

SALAD
80 g rocket
1 English cucumber, julienned
100 g mangetout, sliced in half at an angle
2 sticks celery, thinly sliced lengthways
125 g French beans, blanched
1 x 250 g punnet cherry tomatoes, halved
2 avocados, sliced in thin wedges
a handful of chopped piquant peppers
100 g cashew nuts, roasted and chopped
½ cup chopped chives
6 spring onions, chopped

DRESSING
6 Tbsp olive oil
2 Tbsp red wine vinegar
1 tsp mustard powder
1 clove garlic, chopped
½ small red onion, chopped
¼ cup chopped fresh parsley
2 tsp brown sugar

1. Season the chicken with the chicken spice and sea salt.
2. Mix the honey, lemon juice and zest and olive oil, and pour over the chicken. Leave to marinate overnight.
3. Cook the chicken on the barbecue and slice into strips.
4. Arrange the rocket, cucumber, mangetout, celery, beans, tomatoes, avocados and piquant peppers on a platter. Place the chicken strips in rows on top of the salad. Top with the cashews, chives and spring onions.
5. Whizz the dressing ingredients in a food processor and dress the salad before serving.

Serves 4–6

Herbed potato and caperberry salad

1 kg baby potatoes
12 spring onions, cut at an angle
⅓ cup chopped fresh dill
½ cup chopped fresh flat-leaf parsley
½ cup chopped chives
1 x 135 g jar pickled caperberries, drained, patted dry and halved

DRESSING
¾ cup olive oil
¼ cup red wine vinegar
1 tsp Herbamare® organic herb seasoning salt
freshly ground black pepper to taste
1 Tbsp brown sugar
1 Tbsp Dijon mustard

1. Boil the potatoes in salted water until cooked, but firm. Cut in half and place in a salad bowl.
2. Add the spring onions, dill, parsley, chives and caperberries.
3. Whisk together the dressing ingredients and gently fold into the salad.

TO SERVE IN POTATO SKINS
6 large potatoes
a little olive oil
salt and freshly ground black pepper to taste

1. Preheat the oven to 180 °C.
2. Rub the potatoes with olive oil and season with salt and pepper. Place on a baking tray and bake for 2 hours. Remove and allow to cool.
3. Cut the cooled potatoes in half lengthways and scoop out and discard the insides. Place the skins back in the oven for a further 20 minutes until crispy.
4. Fill with the above salad and serve.

Serves 4–6

Seared tuna Niçoise platter

1 kg fresh tuna loins
a squeeze of fresh lemon juice
sea salt and freshly ground black pepper to taste
a little olive oil

SALAD

1 cup finely sliced fennel
6–8 large radishes, finely sliced
8 Israeli cucumbers, sliced into thin ribbons lengthways using a potato peeler
100 g fine French beans, blanched for a few minutes in boiling water

DRESSING
1 Tbsp chopped fresh flat-leaf parsley
1 clove garlic, crushed
¾ tsp deseeded and chopped fresh red chilli
2 tsp Dijon mustard
½ cup olive oil
2 Tbsp balsamic vinegar
2 Tbsp white wine vinegar

1. Wash the tuna and pat dry. Squeeze over a little lemon juice, and season with salt and pepper.
2. Heat the olive oil in a frying pan and, when very hot, sear the tuna to your preference – rare or medium. When cold, slice into strips lengthways and place on a platter.
3. Layer the salad ingredients next to the tuna.
4. Whisk the dressing ingredients in a blender and dress the salad before serving.

Serves 4–6

Waldorf salad

4 small baby gem lettuce, washed

3 sticks celery, finely sliced

1 large Granny Smith apple, sliced in thin wedges

½ medium pineapple, sliced in thin wedges

55 g dried cranberries, soaked in water to soften and then drained

85 g pecan nuts, lightly toasted and roughly chopped

DRESSING

1 cup good-quality mayonnaise

½ tsp curry powder

¼ cup fresh pineapple juice

2 Tbsp sour cream

¼ tsp sea salt

1. Place the lettuce leaves on a platter and arrange the celery, apple and pineapple on top. Sprinkle over the cranberries.
2. Whisk together the dressing ingredients and dress the salad just before serving.
3. Top with the toasted pecan nuts.

Serves 4–6

Warm asparagus and crumbled feta salad

400 g fresh green asparagus
a squeeze of fresh lemon juice
200 g baby rosa tomatoes
olive oil for drizzling
Herbamare® organic herb seasoning salt to taste
freshly ground black pepper to taste
¼ cup basil pesto (ready-made or see page 60)
200 g feta cheese, crumbled
¼ cup pine nuts, toasted
½ cup chopped fresh basil

1. To cook the perfect asparagus, trim the hard woody stems and wash well in cold water.
   Place the asparagus in salted boiling water with a squeeze of lemon juice.
2. Cook thin-stemmed asparagus for approximately 3 minutes – thicker stems require about
   6 minutes. To check if the asparagus are cooked, remove one from the pot. If the tip bends,
   it is ready. Drain in a colander and refresh under cold water to stop the cooking process.
3. Preheat the oven to 180 °C.
4. Arrange the tomatoes on a baking tray and drizzle with olive oil. Season with the
   seasoning salt and pepper, and roast until just soft. Remove from the oven and drizzle
   with the basil pesto.
5. Sprinkle over the crumbled feta and return to the oven for a few minutes until the feta
   is warm.
6. Arrange the asparagus on a platter. Spoon the tomatoes, feta and pesto over the asparagus.
   Sprinkle with the pine nuts and basil.

VARIATION

Boil the asparagus as in the above recipe. Preheat the oven to 180 °C. Place the asparagus
in an ovenproof dish and dot with small blobs of 75 g softened butter. Sprinkle over ½ cup
finely grated Parmesan cheese and ½ cup flaked and toasted almonds. Warm in the oven
and serve immediately.

Serves 4–6

Quinoa
with sautéed vegetables and goat's cheese

4 sweetcorn cobs
1 Tbsp butter
freshly ground salt
3 Tbsp vegetable oil
1 head fennel, thinly sliced
¾ cup chopped spring onion
1 large red pepper, deseeded and diced
1 tsp chopped fresh parsley
2 Tbsp mirin or white balsamic vinegar sweetened with a little honey
300 g depodded broad beans
250 g quinoa, cooked according to packet instructions
150 g goat's cheese
4 sticks celery, chopped
½ lemon
1 Tbsp chopped fresh mint

1. Remove the corn from the cobs.
2. Heat the butter in a saucepan and sauté the corn for 5 minutes, adding 1 Tbsp salt while cooking. Stir to prevent burning and cook until glassy and slightly crunchy. Remove from the heat and set aside.
3. Heat the vegetable oil in a pan and sauté the fennel, spring onion and red pepper for 5 minutes.
4. Add the parsley and mirin or sweetened vinegar, and season with extra salt to taste. Stir well and, when soft, remove from the heat.
5. Bring a pot of salted water to a rapid boil, and add the beans. Cook for 3–5 minutes, then remove the beans and refresh them under cold running water.
6. Gently peel the outer layer to reveal the bright green bean inside.
7. Place the cooked quinoa in a bowl. Add the sautéed sweetcorn and vegetables and stir to combine. Add the beans.
8. While still warm, fold in the goat's cheese and then add the celery. Squeeze over the lemon and garnish with the fresh mint.

Serves 4–6

Green and red salad
with raspberry vinaigrette

500 g baby spinach
3 large fresh beetroot, peeled and grated
½ red cabbage, shredded
6 fresh figs or 6 dried Turkish figs, halved and then cut into wedges
1 English cucumber, peeled, pips removed and cut into matchsticks
150 g fresh or frozen raspberries, defrosted

DRESSING
¼ cup red wine vinegar
⅓ cup olive oil
⅓ cup canola oil
150 g fresh or frozen raspberries, defrosted
sea salt and freshly ground black pepper to taste

1. Remove the stems from the spinach and arrange on a platter. Arrange the vegetables on top and then top with the raspberries.
2. To make the dressing, blend all the ingredients. Dress the salad just before serving.

Serves 4–6

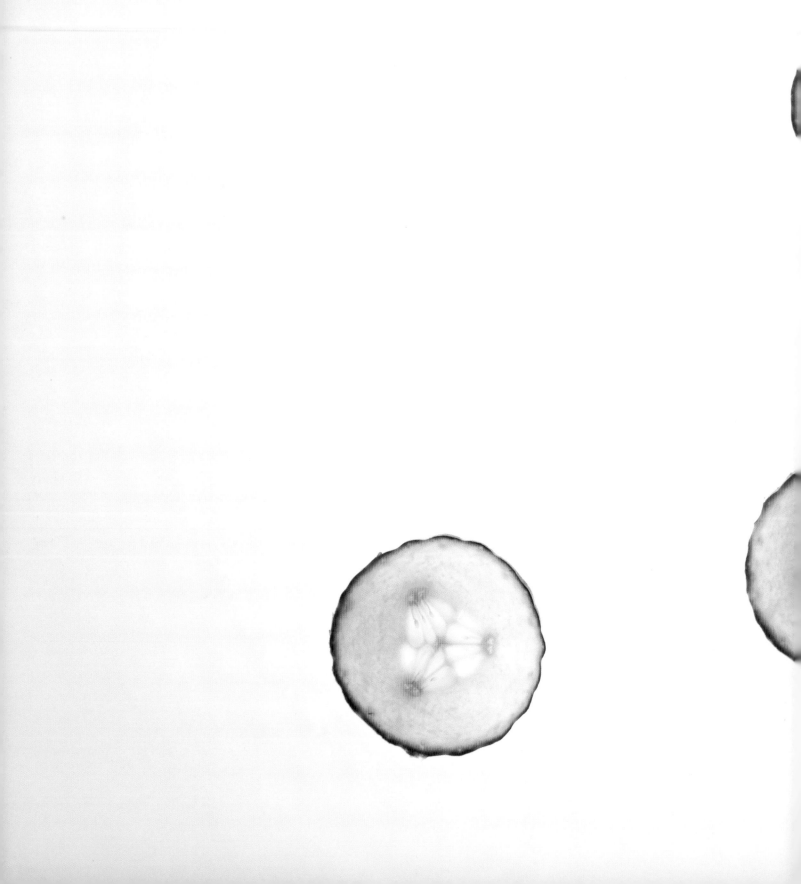

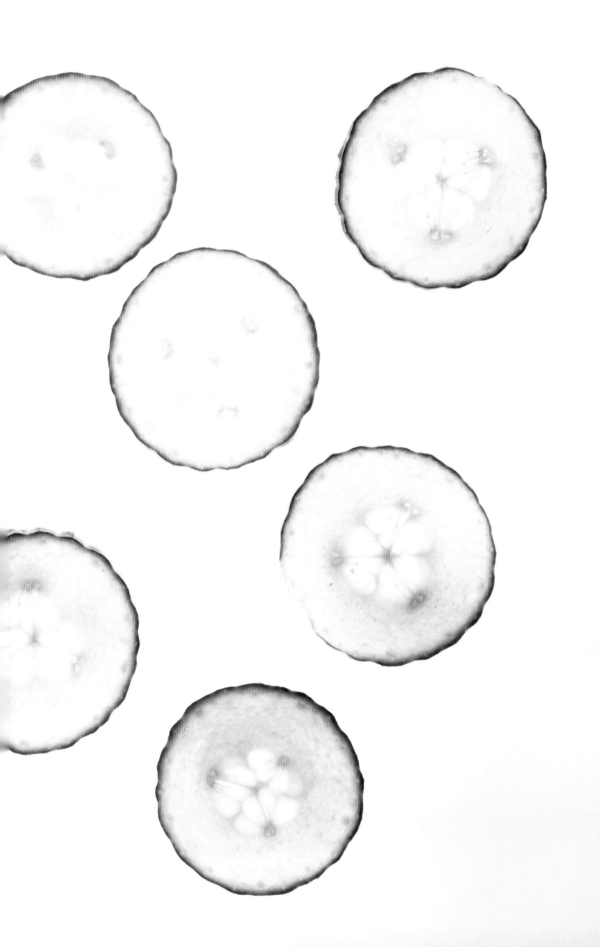

LOVE

Pronounced [luhv]
(Noun) Profoundly tender, passionate affection for another arising out of kinship or personal ties; warm attachment, enthusiasm or devotion; the object of attachment or admiration; *oh, beloved beer batter*. **(Verb tr.)** To hold dear; to cherish; to experience desire for *sashimi*; an object or thing so liked: *cheese!*; to have a strong liking for *thick-cut salted chips*; to take great guilt-free pleasure in *devouring a toasted sandwich*; to need or require. **Important:** Feed your *sweetheart*; share the love; *love to eat*.

SANDWICHES ANY WHICH WAY ...

… toasted, plain, open, closed, in a croissant
or using fresh homemade bread

Toasted three-cheese and tomato

a little butter
4 slices wholewheat bread or 2 croissants
4 slices Emmenthal cheese
4 slices mozzarella cheese
4 slices mature Cheddar cheese
a handful of baby rosa tomatoes, halved
a handful of fresh rocket
Herbamare® organic herb seasoning salt to taste
freshly ground black pepper to taste

1. To make a toasted sandwich, spread butter on the outside of each slice of bread.
2. Divide the sliced cheeses between the sandwiches and top with the halved tomatoes and
   rocket. Sprinkle with seasoning salt and black pepper. Close and toast. Alternatively, place
   the filling inside a soft fresh croissant and heat under the grill until the cheese melts.

Makes 2

Toasted tuna pâté

PÂTÉ
250 g tinned tuna, drained
½ cup fresh cream
125 g smooth cottage cheese
2 tsp fresh lemon juice
1 tsp creamed horseradish
a dash of paprika, ground nutmeg and sea salt to taste

a little butter
4 slices health loaf (see page 80) or 2 croissants
sliced gherkins and piquant peppers

1. Make the pâté the day before. Flake the tuna into the bowl of a food processor and add the
   other ingredients. Blend well and allow to set in the fridge.
2. To make a toasted sandwich, spread butter on the outside of each slice of bread. Spread the
   tuna pâté on two slices, top with sliced gherkins and piquant peppers. Close the sandwich
   and toast. Alternatively, place the filling inside a soft fresh croissant and heat under the grill.

Makes 2

Rare roast beef with caramelised onions

2 onions, thinly sliced
2 Tbsp olive oil
½ cup chutney
1 tsp balsamic vinegar
¼ cup water
a little mayonnaise
2 slices rye or homemade bread (see 'Spread') or 2 croissants
8–10 thin slices roast beef
wholegrain mustard

1. Fry the onions in the olive oil until limp. Add the chutney, balsamic vinegar
   and water, and cook until the mixture thickens. Set aside to cool.
2. Spread a little mayonnaise on each slice of bread and arrange the roast beef on
   top. Spread with the wholegrain mustard and top with the caramelised onions.
   Serve as open sandwiches.

Makes 2

Baked mushroom risotto

250 g assorted dried mushrooms
3 cups boiling water
1 Tbsp olive oil
1 Tbsp butter
1 onion, finely chopped
1 tsp crushed garlic
250 g arborio rice (risotto rice)
½ cup dry white wine
freshly ground black pepper to taste
1 Tbsp chopped fresh thyme
½ cup grated Parmesan cheese

1. Preheat the oven to 190 °C and grease an ovenproof
   dish or saucepan.
2. Rehydrate the mushrooms in 1 cup of the boiling water.
   Drain (keeping the liquid) and set aside.
3. Heat the oil and butter in a frying pan and lightly fry
   the onion, garlic, mushrooms and rice for 5 minutes
   (the rice will become glassy).
4. Add the water from the rehydrated mushrooms, the
   remaining 2 cups of boiling water and the white wine.
   Season with black pepper and add the thyme.
   Cook for 10 minutes.
5. Place the risotto in the greased dish or saucepan
   and fold in the Parmesan.
6. Bake for 30–40 minutes until the rice is cooked through.

Serves 2

Beer-battered fish, chunky salted chips and tartare sauce

500 g hake or any soft white fish, skinned and deboned

fish spice

1 egg

¼ cup sweet beer

sunflower oil for frying

1 cup cake flour

1. Wash the fish and pat dry with paper towels before cutting into 3 cm strips. Season the strips with fish spice, ensuring they are evenly coated.
2. Beat the egg and mix in the beer.
3. Heat the oil in a frying pan, using enough to cover the fish strips. When the oil is sizzling hot, dip the fish strips in the flour and shake off the excess. Then dip in the beer-egg mixture. Fry the strips in the hot oil, turning to brown all over.
4. When the fish is cooked, remove and drain on paper towels or brown paper. Serve with fresh lemon wedges, and the chunky hot chips and tartare sauce below.

CHUNKY CHIPS

4 potatoes, cut in half and then into 2 cm wedges

Trocomare® organic spicy herb seasoning salt

paprika

sunflower oil for frying

sea salt

lemon wedges

1. Season the potato wedges with seasoning salt and paprika.
2. Heat some oil in a large frying pan and add batches of wedges. Fry until the insides of the wedges are cooked and the outsides are golden and crispy.
3. Remove and drain on paper towels.
4. Sprinkle with sea salt and serve with lemon wedges and tartare sauce.

TARTARE SAUCE

1 cup mayonnaise

1 Tbsp chopped fresh parsley

1 tsp chopped fresh dill

3 Tbsp chopped gherkins

2 Tbsp chopped spring onion

a squeeze of fresh lemon juice

sea salt and freshly ground black pepper to taste

1 tsp mustard powder

Mix all the ingredients and chill for a few hours in the fridge before serving with the fish and chips.

Serves 2

Sashimi platter with wasabi pea dip

500 g fresh tuna
500 g fresh salmon

1. Slice the fish into sashimi portions (approximately 3 cm wide) using a sharp knife.
2. Arrange on a platter and serve with the following accompaniments: wasabi pea dip (see below), pickled ginger, pickled daikon, chopped avocado, soy sauce and toasted sesame seeds.

Serves 6–8

WASABI PEA DIP
1 Tbsp olive oil
1 small red onion, chopped
70 g wasabi-coated peas, crushed
¼ cup mayonnaise
½–1 tsp wasabi paste (optional)
1 pickled piquant pepper, chopped
½ tsp chopped garlic
1 Tbsp pickled ginger
salt and freshly ground black pepper to taste

1. Heat the olive oil and sauté the onion for 5 minutes.
2. Remove and place in a blender with the wasabi peas, mayonnaise, wasabi paste (if using), piquant pepper, garlic and pickled ginger, and process until slightly chunky. Season to taste.
3. Serve with salted edamame (see page 176).

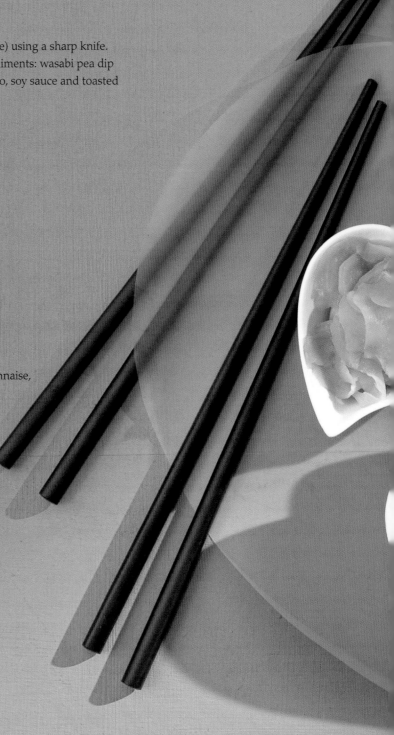

Salted edamame

500 g edamame
2 Tbsp sea salt flakes
50 g sesame seeds, toasted

1. Boil the edamame for 3 minutes in fast boiling water. Remove and drain well.
2. Place the edamame in a serving bowl and sprinkle with the sea salt. Serve hot with the toasted sesame seeds in a small bowl for dipping.

Serves 4–6

Cheese board … for two

On a very large platter or board ideal for two place: wedges of cheese such as Gorgonzola, Emmenthal, goat's cheese, ripe Camembert, ripe Brie … Adorn with ginger rounds (see page 353), lavender and honey mustard (see page 43), marmalade, preserves … Heap on sliced fresh figs, dates, granadillas, grapes … And serve with a warm crunchy fig tart (see page 179).

Warm crunchy fig tart

18 fresh figs, halved
1 cup fresh blueberries
¾ cup treacle sugar
100 g butter, softened
1½ cups cornflakes
⅔ cup oats
½ cup cake flour

1. Preheat the oven to 180 °C and grease a 25 cm-diameter
   pie dish. Arrange the fruit in the pie dish.
2. Using a beater, combine the treacle sugar and butter.
   Add the remaining ingredients and mix well.
3. Arrange on top of the fruit.
4. Bake for 40–45 minutes until golden brown and crisp.
5. Serve warm with fresh cream or custard, or with a
   cheeseboard (see page 176).

(Note: If figs are not in season, replace with 4 large peaches,
peeled, stoned and thinly sliced in segments, and 4 medium
nectarines, peeled, stoned and thinly sliced in segments.)

Mocha whoopie pies

125 g unsalted butter, softened
1 packed cup treacle sugar
1 large egg, at room temperature
2 cups cake flour
⅔ cup cocoa powder
1 tsp baking powder
½ tsp bicarbonate of soda
½ tsp salt
1¼ cups buttermilk
1 tsp vanilla essence

MOCHA CREAM FILLING
2½ cups icing sugar, sifted
100 g butter, softened
2 heaped tsp strong coffee granules mixed with a little water to form a paste
¼ cup thick fresh cream
a little milk, if needed

1. Preheat the oven to 180 °C and line two baking trays with baking paper.
2. Beat the butter and sugar until light and fluffy, add the egg and beat until combined.
3. In a separate bowl, sift the dry ingredients together. Stir the dry ingredients, alternating with the buttermilk, into the sugar mixture. Mix in the vanilla essence.
4. Using a 15 mm nozzle, pipe rounds of the batter 5 cm apart onto the baking trays.
5. Bake for 10 minutes until the edges appear firm. Allow to cool on the baking trays for 5 minutes, before transferring to a wire rack to cool thoroughly.
6. In the meantime, make the mocha cream filling. Beat the icing sugar and butter until crumbly. Add the coffee paste and cream, beating slowly until combined. Add a little milk if the filling becomes too thick.
7. Take one round, spread the flat side with the mocha cream filling using a knife or piping bag and top with another round, flat-side down to form a sandwich.

Makes 24

I ♡ scones …

2 cups cake flour
4 level tsp baking powder
1 Tbsp sugar
a pinch of salt
125 g butter, softened
2 eggs, at room temperature
½ cup milk

1. Preheat the oven to 190 °C and grease a baking tray.
2. Sift the flour, baking powder, sugar and salt into a bowl.
   With your fingertips, rub the butter into the flour mixture.
3. In a separate bowl, beat one egg with the milk, and add
   to the flour mixture. Mix to form a soft dough.
   If the mixture is too wet, rub your hands in a little
   flour as you knead the dough.
4. On a floured board, roll the dough into a flat sheet,
   approximately 3 cm thick. With a heart-shaped cutter
   (or a round 6–7 cm cutter), cut out eight scones.
5. Lightly beat the remaining egg and brush onto the scones.
   Place on the baking tray and bake for 12–15 minutes until lightly brown.
6. Serve with butter, fresh cream and jam.

Makes 8

Pronounced [spahys]

(Noun) Any of various pungent, aromatic plant substances, such as paprika, cinnamon or nutmeg, used to flavour foods or beverages; an ingredient that adds zest or zing. **(Verb tr.)** To season with spices; to incorporate oomph; to liven up with *peri-peri*; to coat with a *warm chilli glaze and mustard fruit*; to invigorate with *curry paste*; to fill with ardour; to inspire; to ignite sparkles in your mouth. **Suggested accompaniment:** Water or milk.

Warmed Camembert
with syrupy chilli glaze and mustard fruit

300 g Camembert
400 g mustard fruit
(Italian mostarda fruit)

GLAZE (do not double this recipe)
1 cup sugar
½ cup water
½ fresh chilli, deseeded and
   finely chopped

1. Place the Camembert on a platter.
2. Bring the sugar, water and chilli
   to the boil in a saucepan, stirring
   until it boils.
3. Once boiling, stop stirring and allow
   the mixture to boil rapidly until it
   becomes light golden brown.
4. Remove from the stove – do not
   stir – and pour over the cheese
   immediately.
5. When set, serve with the Italian
   mustard fruit.

Serves 4–6

Marinated chilli salmon

1 red onion, finely sliced
1 Tbsp fresh lemon juice
1 cup olive oil
250 g smoked salmon
2 fresh red chillies, deseeded
   and chopped
freshly ground black pepper to taste

1. Marinate the red onion in the lemon
   juice and olive oil for 10 minutes.
2. Chop the smoked salmon into
   small pieces and combine with
   the red onion and lemon juice.
   Add the chillies.
3. Season with black pepper.
4. Mix well and refrigerate in an
   airtight container for up to a week.
5. Serve with fresh bread.

Serves 4–6

Portuguese-style peri-peri chicken

PERI-PERI SAUCE
3 fresh chillies, chopped
1 Tbsp paprika
2 tsp peri-peri powder
2 cloves garlic, chopped
¾ cup olive oil

1.5 kg spatchcock chicken
sea salt and freshly ground black pepper to taste
juice and grated rind of 1 lemon
garlic flakes for sprinkling

1. To make the peri-peri sauce, mix all the ingredients and leave to stand for a few hours.
2. Preheat the oven to 220 °C.
3. Clean the chicken well. Season with salt and pepper, and rub with the lemon juice and rind.
4. Par-grill the chicken for 30–35 minutes, then remove from the oven.
5. Place on a barbecue, baste with the peri-peri sauce and sprinkle with garlic flakes.
6. Cook until the chicken is brown and crispy.
7. Alternatively, baste and return to the oven uncovered to cook for about 20 minutes.

Serves 2–4

Chicken burgers with peri mayonnaise

Prepare chicken breast fillets according to the chicken salad recipe on page 148. Do not slice the chicken into long thin strips. Place on a burger bun or toasted ciabatta roll with peri mayonnaise (see below), shredded lettuce and thinly sliced red onion rings.

PERI MAYONNAISE
Combine good-quality mayonnaise with peri-peri sauce (see page 191) to taste, or use ready-made perinaise.

Serves 4

Spicy beef bunny chow

¼ cup olive oil
1 onion, chopped
4 leeks, chopped
2 cloves garlic, chopped
3 large carrots, grated
200 g rosa tomatoes, halved
1 kg beef, cut into 1 cm cubes
salt and freshly ground black pepper to taste
2 Tbsp ground cumin
2 Tbsp ground coriander
5 Tbsp Worcestershire sauce
1 tsp chilli flakes
1 heaped tsp dried thyme
1 heaped tsp dried parsley
1–2 fresh green chillies, deseeded and chopped
2 cups tomato sauce
1 tsp smoked paprika
1 x 400 g tin cannellini beans, drained and washed
3 cups boiling water
2 loaves good-quality bread with a strong crust or 4 round crispy Italian rolls
chopped fresh parsley for garnishing

1. Heat half of the olive oil in a large frying pan. Sauté the onion, leeks, garlic, carrots and tomatoes until soft. Remove from the pan and set aside.
2. In the same pan, heat the remaining olive oil over a high heat and brown the beef. Season with salt and pepper, and add the cumin, coriander and Worcestershire sauce. Add the chilli flakes, thyme, parsley, chillies, tomato sauce and paprika, and sauté for 15–20 minutes until the meat is tender and the sauce has thickened, becoming gooey.
3. Add the sautéed vegetables and cannellini beans, and stir. Add the boiling water and allow to simmer, uncovered, until reduced and saucy.
4. Cut the loaves of bread in half or cut the tops off the rolls, and scoop out some of the inside to make a 'bowl'. Stand the loaves or rolls on a plate and fill with the beef and sauce.
5. Garnish with chopped parsley before serving. Be sure to use the bread to mop up the sauce!

Serves 4

Brinjal curry

1 kg baby brinjals, washed and halved
oil for sautéing
1 medium onion, chopped
1 clove garlic, crushed
½ tsp coarse salt
1 cinnamon stick
1 bay leaf
2–3 green cardamom pods
2 star anise
a few curry leaves
½ tsp turmeric
2 Tbsp curry powder
3 medium tomatoes, peeled and grated (peel the tomatoes by soaking
   them for a few minutes in boiled water until the skins soften)
1 cup boiling water
2 tsp ground cumin
1 Tbsp garam masala
chopped fresh coriander for serving

1. Soak the brinjal halves in salted water for about 10 minutes to take away the bitterness.
   Rinse well.
2. Heat some oil in a large saucepan and sauté the onion. Add the garlic, salt and all the spices,
   except the cumin and garam masala. Mix well.
3. Add the brinjals and cook for 5 minutes, then add the tomatoes and boiling water.
   Cook, covered, until the brinjals are soft. Stir in the cumin and garam masala.
4. Serve garnished with chopped coriander.

Serves 4–6

Warm white chocolate pudding
with chilli–chocolate centre

150 g good-quality white chocolate
60 g butter
1 Tbsp fresh cream
3 eggs
75 g castor sugar
3 Tbsp cake flour, sifted
200 g Lindt Excellence Chili Noir or equivalent

CHOCOLATE SAUCE
100 g good-quality white chocolate
¼ cup fresh cream
½ tsp vanilla essence

1. Preheat the oven to 180 °C. Grease eight ramekins (8 cm high x 4.5 cm wide).
2. Melt the white chocolate, butter and cream in a double boiler.
3. In a separate bowl, beat the eggs and castor sugar until pale. Add the flour.
   Stir in the white chocolate mixture.
4. Pour the mixture into the ramekins and place a piece of chilli chocolate in each.
5. Bake for 12–15 minutes until just golden. The pudding must be moist inside.
6. To make the chocolate sauce, melt the chocolate and cream in a double boiler until
   well combined, and then stir in the vanilla essence.
7. Serve the puddings in the ramekins or allow to cool completely before removing.
8. To serve warm, reheat on a baking tray for a few minutes. Prick each pudding with
   a fork and pour over the chocolate sauce.

Makes 8

Pronounced [siz-*uhl*]

(Verb tr.) To cook food so that it makes a hissing sound; to prepare ingredients using a griddle; to sear food, creating crispy crusts without charring; to *sizzle tender steaks*. **(Verb past part.)** *The sausages sizzled on the barbecue; the chicken livers sizzled in the griddle pan.* **(Noun)** A frying noise; the hissing and splattering sound of something frying, sautéing or being seared *with a little olive oil and freshly ground black pepper*; laid-back fare; chill-out chow; the sound of summer. **(Adv.)** Sizzlingly. **Synonyms:** Sputter; spatter; crackle; hiss.

SIZZLE

Grilled chicken livers and crispy panzanella salad

¼ cup olive oil
1 loaf ciabatta, cut into 1 cm-thick slices
2 onions, sliced into rings
1 tsp chilli powder
1 tsp seasoning salt
1 Tbsp chopped fresh origanum
¾ cup chopped fresh Italian flat-leaf parsley
400 g portobello mushrooms, wiped with damp towel (not washed)
500 g chicken livers, any sinews or black spots removed
150 g rosa tomatoes, halved
salt and freshly ground black pepper to taste
1 lemon
fresh basil leaves for garnishing

1. Brush a little olive oil onto a flat-grill gas barbecue or a griddle pan on the stove.
2. Brush the ciabatta slices with olive oil and brown them over a high heat until golden and crisp. Remove and drain on paper towels.
3. Heat another 2 Tbsp olive oil and sauté the onion rings with the chilli powder, seasoning salt, origanum and ¼ cup parsley. Add the mushrooms and cook until browned. Transfer the mixture to a bowl and place in a warming drawer to keep warm.
4. Heat a little more olive oil and grill the chicken livers until cooked through.
5. Arrange the livers on a platter, throw over the warm mushroom mixture and add the tomatoes and toasted ciabatta slices. Top with the remaining parsley, season with salt and pepper, drizzle with a little olive oil and squeeze over the juice of the lemon.
6. Garnish with fresh basil leaves and serve immediately.

Serves 4–6

Grilled halloumi, chickpea and watercress salad

180 g halloumi, cut into 2 cm-thick slices
½ cup cake flour
120 g thin spring onions, trimmed
1 x 400 g tin chickpeas, drained
150 g fresh petits pois, blanched
100 g mixed rocket, watercress and baby leaf spinach
2 lemons, cut into small wedges

DRESSING
½ cup olive oil
½ cup fresh lemon juice
1 tsp sugar
sea salt and freshly ground black pepper to taste

1. Coat the halloumi with the flour and shake off the excess.
2. Heat a griddle pan greased with non-stick cooking spray and grill the cheese slices for approximately 2 minutes each side. Remove and set aside.
3. Lightly grill the spring onions over a barbecue or in the pan.
4. Arrange the chickpeas, petits pois, spring onions and mixed greens on a platter and top with the halloumi. Garnish with lemon wedges.
5. Whisk the dressing ingredients, pour over the salad and serve immediately.

Serves 4–6

Barbecue-basted beef and vegetarian kebabs

BEEF KEBABS

½ tsp cayenne pepper

1 tsp each of paprika and garlic salt

1 cup tomato sauce

2 Tbsp treacle sugar

¼ cup Worcestershire sauce

1 large onion, chopped

1 Tbsp mustard powder

1 kg rib-eye steak, thickly cubed

2 sweetcorn cobs

1 tsp coarse salt plus extra to taste

1 red pepper, halved and deseeded

16–20 baby pearl onions, peeled

wooden skewers (soak in water before using)

1. Combine the cayenne pepper, paprika, garlic salt, tomato sauce, sugar, Worcestershire sauce, onion and mustard powder. (Use this marinade to baste the vegetarian kebabs below.) Pour over the steak and marinate in a Ziploc™ bag in the fridge overnight. Shake the bag occasionally.
2. Parboil the corn cobs in salted water and cut into 2 cm-thick rings.
3. Cut the red pepper into thick squares.
4. To make the kebabs, thread the ingredients onto the skewers as follows: meat, corn, meat, red pepper, meat, pearl onion, meat. Brush with the leftover marinade and sprinkle with salt.
5. Grill over a medium heat, turning until the meat is cooked to your preference.

VEGETARIAN KEBABS

6 baby beetroots, peeled

500 g butternut, peeled and cubed

coarse salt and freshly ground black pepper to taste

½ cup olive oil

2 yellow peppers, halved and deseeded

2 red onions, each cut into 6 wedges

250 g brown mushrooms, wiped with damp paper towels and cut into thick chunks

Herbamare® organic herb seasoning salt to taste

wooden skewers (soak in water before using)

1. Season the beetroot and butternut with salt and pepper. Toss in a little olive oil and roast on a baking tray until cooked but still firm.
2. Cut the yellow peppers into thick squares and toss with the red onions and mushrooms in a little olive oil. Season with Herbamare® and black pepper.
3. Thread the vegetables alternately onto the skewers and baste with the marinade if desired.
4. Grill over a medium heat until the vegetables are firm but cooked. Eat straight off the skewers or toss in a salad with fresh greens, and drizzle with olive oil and balsamic vinegar.

Makes 4–6 of each

Grilled baguette sausage dog

1–2 heads garlic
1 cup good-quality red wine
4 onions, sliced
2 level tsp brown sugar
12 beef or chicken sausages
3 long baguettes, each cut into four equal-sized pieces

1. Peel and chop the garlic. Cook the garlic, red wine, onions and sugar in a saucepan over a medium heat to reduce. Stir continuously to avoid burning. When reduced and sticky, remove and set aside to cool.
2. Grill the sausages on the barbecue over a medium heat.
3. Slice open the baguette pieces and toast on the barbecue.
4. Serve the sausages in the baguettes with the caramelised onions, pickled cucumbers (see page 32) and an avocado salsa (see page 59). Alternatively, serve the sausages with a sweet chilli dipping sauce and crispy potato wedges (see page 309).

Serves 8–10

Sticky glazed salmon steaks
with teriyaki corn

4 x 250 g fresh Scottish or Norwegian salmon steaks
juice of ½ lime
sea salt and freshly ground black pepper to taste
¼ tsp garlic flakes
¼ tsp chopped fresh parsley
Ponzu sauce for serving

GLAZE
¼ cup soy sauce
¾ cup sweet chilli sauce
3 Tbsp honey
½ tsp sesame oil

1. Rinse the salmon and pat dry. Place the fish skin-side down on a greased baking tray and squeeze over the lime juice. Season with salt and pepper, and sprinkle over the garlic flakes and parsley.
2. Mix together the glaze ingredients and pour over the salmon. Refrigerate for a few hours before cooking on the barbecue for 4–6 minutes, depending on how rare you like your salmon. While cooking, baste with the glaze.
3. Serve the salmon with Ponzu sauce and the following teriyaki corn.

TERIYAKI CORN
2 Tbsp teriyaki sauce
2 Tbsp soy sauce
1 Tbsp sesame oil
12 x mini corn cobs
wooden skewers (soaked for 30 minutes in water)

1. Whisk the teriyaki sauce, soy sauce and sesame oil in a bowl.
2. Place the mini corn cobs in the marinade, ensuring they are all covered, and marinate for 1 hour.
3. Place each corn on a wooden skewer and cook over an open flame, turning constantly until slightly charred.

Serves 4

Roasted fruit
with elderflower sorbet

½ cup fresh lime juice

3 Tbsp honey

⅓ cup melted butter

4 mangoes, outer rounded edges removed and thickly sliced

2 pineapples, peeled and sliced into thick rings or long slices

1 coconut, meat roughly broken into shards

1. Whisk together the lime juice, honey and melted butter, and use to brush the fruit (on both sides).
2. Grill on the barbecue until nicely roasted.
3. Serve with the following elderflower sorbet.

ELDERFLOWER SORBET

150 ml elderflower syrup

3 egg whites

chopped fresh mint to taste

1 kg crushed ice

extra fresh mint for garnishing

1. Whizz all the ingredients in a blender.
2. Place in a shallow dish and set in the freezer. Remove just before serving and scrape into glasses.
3. Garnish with fresh mint.

Serves 4–6

Roasted bananas
with crushed coconut biscuits, caramel and rum

8 Tennis™ or coconut tea biscuits, crushed
4 heaped Tbsp caramel (you can make
   caramel by boiling and reducing
   a tin of condensed milk)
1 tot rum
4 ripe bananas (do not peel)

1. Mix the biscuits, caramel and rum.
2. Cut slits lengthways in the banana
   skins and spoon the caramel mixture
   into the slits.
3. Wrap each banana in foil, shiny-side
   inwards, and cook over an open
   flame for 10–12 minutes until soft.

Serves 4

Roasted bananas
with chocolate and coconut

16 squares good-quality milk
   chocolate, chopped
¼ cup desiccated coconut
a pinch of coarse salt
4 ripe bananas (do not peel)

1. Mix the chocolate, coconut and salt.
2. Cut slits lengthways in the banana
   skins and spoon the chocolate
   mixture into the slits.
3. Wrap each banana in foil, shiny-side
   inwards, and cook over an open
   flame for 10–12 minutes until soft.

Serves 4

Mini cake pops

The perfect pop to pass around after the barbecue.

1 x 600 g chocolate or vanilla instant
   cake mix (plus the ingredients listed
   on the box)
453 g instant frosting (Pillsbury)
450 g white or milk chocolate
48 candy sticks

1. Grease and line a 23 x 23 x 5 cm
   square cake tin.
2. Bake the cake mix according to the
   packet instructions. Allow to cool
   completely and trim or grate off the
   brown edges.
3. Crumble the cake into a bowl either
   by hand or using a food processor
   until it resembles breadcrumbs.
4. Mix three-quarters of the tub
   of instant frosting into the cake
   crumbs and combine until all the
   icing is absorbed into the cake.
   Roll this mixture into balls
   (approximately the size of ping-pong
   balls) and place in the fridge for
   1 hour to firm up.
5. Melt the chocolate in the microwave
   on a low heat or in a double boiler.
6. Insert a candy stick into each ball
   and dip into the melted chocolate.
   Stand in a cup to dry.
7. Make as many cake pops as needed
   and freeze the remaining uncoated
   balls. Keep the coated balls in an
   airtight container for up to 1 week.

Makes 48

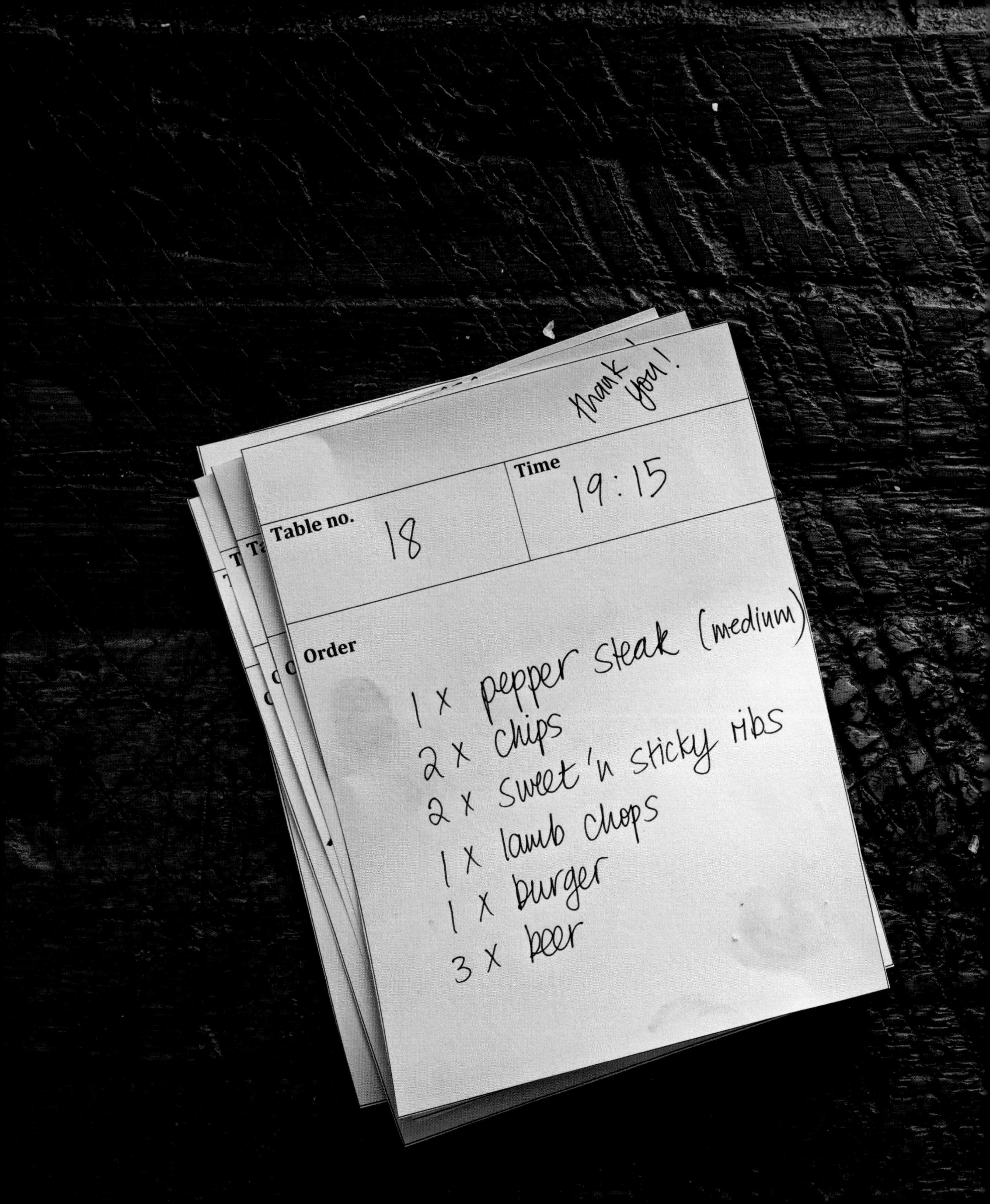

Thank you!

Table no.	18	Time	19:15

Order

1 x pepper steak (medium)
2 x chips
2 x sweet 'n sticky ribs
1 x lamb chops
1 x burger
3 x beer

CLEAVE

Pronounced [kleev]
(Verb tr.) To split with a sharp instrument; to make or accomplish by cutting; to carve a *rack of lamb*; to score a *fillet*.
(Verb) Open, slice; sever; stand by; be true to; be devoted to the *perfect pink piece of pepper steak*; to cling to the aroma of *rosemary-infused chops*; to split *sticky barbecued ribs*; to mould *handmade beef patties*; to eat carnivorously. **Tip:** Keep a stock of toothpicks.

Beef carpaccio
with creamed horseradish sauce

1 kg beef fillet, well-hung and matured
2 Tbsp olive oil
2 Tbsp coarse salt
freshly ground black pepper to taste
a handful of fresh rocket

HORSERADISH SAUCE
1 cup creamed horseradish
½ cup mayonnaise
1 tsp fresh lemon juice
1 tsp sea salt
1 tsp freshly ground black pepper
2 Tbsp chopped chives

1. Wash the fillet well and pat dry. Wrap tightly in clingfilm and freeze.
2. Make the horseradish sauce by whisking all the ingredients together. Chill in the fridge.
3. Remove the fillet and slice paper-thin using an electric slicer, bread slicer or very sharp carving knife.
4. Place the beef on a platter. Cover the platter with clingfilm and place in the fridge until ready to serve.
5. Before serving, brush the beef with olive oil and drizzle over the horseradish sauce.
6. Garnish with rock salt, black pepper and rocket.

Serves 8–10

Sticky and sweet ribs

Prepare these the day before and leave to marinate overnight.

2.5 kg beef short ribs, trimmed
and washed
2 Tbsp fresh lime juice
¼ cup treacle sugar
½ cup fresh lemon juice
5 tsp mustard powder
5 Tbsp Worcestershire sauce
1½ Tbsp paprika
2½ cups chutney

1. Place the ribs in an ovenproof dish.
2. Whisk all the remaining ingredients
   together and pour over the ribs. Cover
   and marinate in the fridge overnight.
3. When ready to cook, preheat the oven
   to 190 °C.
4. Cook the ribs, covered, in the
   marinade for 1 hour.
5. Reduce the temperature to 180 °C
   and roast, uncovered, for a further
   1–1½ hours until tender. If you prefer,
   you can barbecue the ribs after the
   first roasting.

Serves 4–6

The perfect pepper steak

2 Tbsp freshly ground black pepper
2 tsp meat spice
1 kg rib-eye steak, well hung, matured and tenderised, cut 0.75 cm thick
200 g butter or margarine
2 cups water
1 cup Worcestershire sauce
1 baguette

1. Mix the pepper and meat spice and press into the steak.
2. Heat a wok on high, and add the butter or margarine, 1½ cups water and the Worcestershire sauce. Cook until the mixture reduces.
3. Add the remaining ½ cup water and simmer until the sauce thickens.
4. Add the steaks and simmer with the lid on until cooked to your preference (rare, medium or well-done). Baste occasionally.
5. When cooked, slice the steaks into thick pieces and arrange on a platter.
6. Drizzle over the sauce. Serve with chunks of baguette to mop up the sauce!

Serves 4

Scotch fillet
with chimichurri sauce

Prepare this the day before and marinate overnight.

2.5 kg Scotch fillet, trimmed and washed
1 cup fresh lemon juice
1 onion, chopped
2 Tbsp chopped fresh origanum
½ cup soy sauce
1 tsp freshly ground black pepper
2 cloves garlic, halved
garlic and herb salt to taste

CHIMICHURRI SAUCE
¼ cup chopped fresh basil
2 cloves garlic
1 cup chopped Italian flat-leaf parsley
¼ cup fresh lemon juice
¾ cup olive oil
freshly ground black pepper to taste
100 g spring onions, chopped
2 Tbsp chopped fresh origanum
3 Tbsp red wine vinegar
1 slice white bread

1. Place the fillet in a dish.
2. Mix the lemon juice, onion, origanum, soy sauce and pepper, and pour over the fillet.
3. Pierce the fillet and push the garlic halves into the slits. Sprinkle over the garlic and herb salt. Leave to marinate overnight in the fridge.
4. To make the sauce, roughly chop all the sauce ingredients in a food processor. Adjust seasoning and allow to stand for a few hours before serving.
5. When ready to cook, remove the fillet from the marinade and cook on a preheated barbecue until medium-rare. Alternatively, preheat the oven to 190 °C and cook the fillet, uncovered, for approximately 40 minutes.
6. Serve the fillet with the sauce on side.

Serves 4

Handmade burger patties

6 tomatoes
1.5 kg lean mince
3 slices brown bread, soaked in a little water
½ tsp freshly ground black pepper
sea salt to taste
2 tsp beef stock powder
2 apples, peeled and grated
½ cup cold water
½ tsp crushed garlic
1 tsp chopped fresh parsley

1. Soak the tomatoes in boiling water until the skins can be easily removed. Peel and chop finely.
2. Combine with the remaining ingredients in a bowl.
3. Shape into patties and place in the freezer for 2–3 hours.
4. Remove from the freezer and grill on the barbecue or in a hot skillet until cooked according to preference.
5. Serve with fried onion rings, relishes and fresh burger buns.

Makes approximately 20

Cider chicken rules

1 whole chicken
1 x 340 ml can sweet cider
2 Tbsp olive oil
salt and freshly ground black pepper to taste
1 Tbsp chicken stock powder
2 Golden Delicious apples, cored and cut into quarters
a few sprigs of fresh thyme for garnishing

1. Preheat the oven to 200 °C.
2. Rub the chicken with a quarter of the cider (approximately 80 ml) and the olive oil. Season with salt and pepper.
3. Place the opened cider can in the centre of a roasting pan and position the chicken cavity over the can, so that the chicken is standing upright.
4. Cook for 1 hour. Remove the chicken from the pan.
5. Over a medium heat, deglaze the pan by adding the stock powder and the remaining cider in the can. Stir to form a gravy.
6. Sauté the apples in the gravy for a few minutes.
7. Pour the gravy over the chicken or serve on the side. Garnish with thyme.

Serves 4

Poussin
with onion medley stuffing

50 g hazelnuts, shelled and coarsely chopped
2 Tbsp olive oil
1 large red onion, cut into thin wedges
300 g baby leeks, chopped
12 pickling onions, quartered
1 heaped tsp chopped garlic
salt and freshly ground black pepper to taste
1 Tbsp chopped fresh thyme
2 poussin (baby chickens)
chicken spice for seasoning
1 small lemon, cut into thin slices
3 Tbsp fresh lemon juice
2 tsp mustard powder
2 tsp Dijon mustard
2 Tbsp fresh breadcrumbs
extra olive oil for brushing
chopped fresh parsley for serving

1. Preheat the oven to 180 °C and lightly toast the hazelnuts.
2. Spray a roasting pan with non-stick cooking spray and set aside.
3. Heat the olive oil in a frying pan. Sauté the red onion, leeks, pickling onions and garlic for 10–15 minutes. Add salt and pepper to taste and 2 tsp thyme.
4. Spread a quarter of the onion mixture in the bottom of the prepared roasting pan.
5. Season the chickens with salt, pepper and chicken spice. Lift the skins and insert the lemon slices.
6. In a bowl, mix the lemon juice, mustard powder, Dijon mustard, breadcrumbs and remaining thyme. Add half of the onion mixture and the toasted hazelnuts. Place this mixture in the chicken cavities, and place the chickens in the roasting pan. Cover with the remaining onion mixture, then cover with clingfilm and refrigerate for 1 hour.
7. When ready to cook, preheat the oven to 200 °C. Discard the clingfilm and cook the chickens for 45 minutes. Remove the pan from the oven and give it a gentle shake – do not turn the chickens.
8. Brush the chickens with extra olive oil, cover with foil, shiny-side inwards and return to the oven. Cook for a further 15–20 minutes.
9. Garnish with chopped parsley before serving.

Serves 4

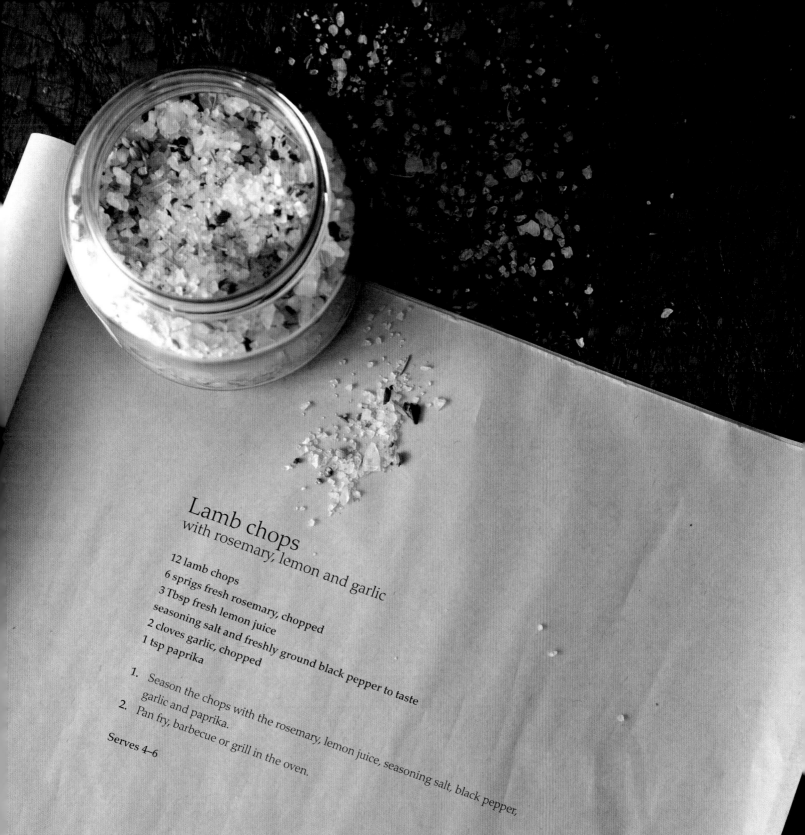

Lamb chops
with rosemary, lemon and garlic

12 lamb chops
6 sprigs fresh rosemary, chopped
3 Tbsp fresh lemon juice
seasoning salt and freshly ground black pepper to taste
2 cloves garlic, chopped
1 tsp paprika

1. Season the chops with the rosemary, lemon juice, seasoning salt, black pepper, garlic and paprika.
2. Pan fry, barbecue or grill in the oven.

Serves 4–6

Rack of lamb
with wasabi–sesame crust and wine reduction
Prepare this the day before and marinate overnight.

4 racks of lamb, 2–3 ribs on each rack, French trimmed
freshly ground black pepper to taste
1 Tbsp fresh lemon juice
2 tsp chopped lemongrass
2 tsp chopped fresh coriander
1 tsp soy sauce
2 Tbsp crushed garlic
2 Tbsp rice wine vinegar
3 Tbsp olive oil
1 Tbsp wasabi powder
1 tsp sesame oil
2 Tbsp white sesame seeds
2 Tbsp black sesame seeds
1 Tbsp water

STICKY LAMB REDUCTION
1 cup lamb stock
½ cup red wine
¼ cup brown sugar

1. Season the lamb with black pepper.
2. Mix the lemon juice, lemongrass, coriander, soy sauce, garlic, rice wine vinegar and olive oil, and rub on the lamb.
3. Place the racks in a dish, flesh side up, with the bones at the bottom.
4. Mix the wasabi powder, sesame oil, sesame seeds and water to form a paste. Brush the lamb with the paste and press it into the flesh. Cover and marinate in the fridge overnight.
5. When ready to cook, preheat the oven to 200 °C. Place the racks in a roasting pan and cook for 20–25 minutes until brown (the sesame crust will look quite dark).
6. Remove from the oven, cover with foil and cook at 180 °C until cooked through according to preference.
7. To make the reduction, bring the lamb stock, red wine and sugar to the boil in a saucepan. Reduce the heat and simmer until the mixture becomes thick and syrupy. Serve on the side.

Serves 4

Lamb
with pomegranate reduction

You can use ready-made pomegranate reduction if you'd prefer.

1.8 kg shoulder of lamb, trimmed and washed
¼ cup olive oil
sea salt and crushed pink peppercorns to taste
pomegranate arils for garnishing

POMEGRANATE REDUCTION
2 cups pomegranate juice
¼ cup treacle sugar
2 Tbsp balsamic vinegar

1. Preheat the oven to 200 °C.
2. Place the lamb in a roasting pan. Rub with the olive oil, sea salt and pink peppercorns. Roast, uncovered, for approximately 40 minutes, turning regularly.
3. Make the pomegranate reduction by boiling all the ingredients in a saucepan until the mixture reduces.
4. Remove the lamb from the oven and add the pomegranate reduction. Cover with foil, shiny-side facing inwards. Lower the temperature to 180 °C and roast the lamb for a further 1 hour, turning and basting every 20 minutes.
5. Garnish with pomegranate arils befrore serving.

Serves 4–6

FOOD AND COOKERY.

Pronounced [im-i-*gruh*nt]

(Noun) One that immigrates; a person who comes to a country to take up permanent residence; an organism found in a new habitat; food from afar; *geographic gastronomy*; a *culinary compass*; a journey from the kitchen door to *faraway fare*.

Roast Gazpacho
with rustic salsa

2.5 kg ripe roma tomatoes, halved
125 g baby leeks, trimmed and sliced in half lengthways
2 large red peppers, deseeded and quartered
2 cloves garlic, halved
3 Tbsp olive oil
Herbamare® organic herb seasoning salt to taste
2 English cucumbers, coarsely chopped
¼ cup fresh lemon juice
1 Tbsp olive oil
2 tsp brown sugar
2 tsp Tabasco® sauce
approximately 1 tsp garlic pepper seasoning
sea salt and freshly ground black pepper to taste

1. Preheat the oven to 180 °C. Cover a large baking tray with foil, shiny-side down, and spray the foil with olive oil cooking spray.
2. Place the tomatoes, leeks, red peppers and garlic on the tray, and brush with the olive oil. Sprinkle with seasoning salt and roast for 10–15 minutes until the tomatoes are just soft (if they become too soft they will be watery). Remove from the oven and allow to cool.
3. Remove the skin from the tomatoes and place the flesh in a large bowl.
4. Coarsely chop the red pepper and add to the bowl along with the leeks, garlic and cucumber.
5. Blend in a food processor until slightly chunky (not smooth). Add the lemon juice, olive oil, brown sugar, Tabasco® sauce and garlic pepper seasoning. Blend again until mixed through (keep the mixture chunky) and season to taste.
6. Chill in the fridge for a few hours. Serve with the salsa below.

SALSA
80 g spring onions, chopped
2 large yellow peppers, deseeded and finely chopped
1 English cucumber, finely chopped
1 avocado, chopped
fresh lemon juice to taste
a few sprigs chervil or fresh parsley

1. Mix the spring onions, peppers, cucumber and avocado in a bowl. Sprinkle with lemon juice and garnish with chervil or parsley.
2. Spoon over the Gazpacho or serve on the side.

Serves 10–12

Warm Thai beef salad

1 kg sirloin or fillet steak
sea salt and freshly ground black pepper to taste
a little olive oil
1 cucumber, chopped
1 x 250 g punnet baby rosa tomatoes, halved

SALAD
2 red onions, sliced in thin rings
½ fresh red chilli, deseeded and thinly sliced
10 spring onions, sliced at an angle
1 Tbsp chopped fresh parsley
½ cup chopped fresh coriander
1 tsp finely grated fresh ginger
a little olive oil

MARINADE
2 Tbsp fish sauce
2 tsp palm sugar
3 Tbsp red wine vinegar
2 Tbsp avocado oil
1 tsp grated fresh ginger

1. Place all the salad ingredients in a bowl, drizzling over a little olive oil.
2. Combine the marinade ingredients and pour over the salad.
   Leave to marinate for approximately 30 minutes.
3. Season the steak with salt and pepper.
4. Heat a little olive oil in a griddle pan and fry the steaks until rare or medium-rare.
5. Slice the hot steak into thick strips.
6. Place the cucumber and tomatoes on a platter and top with the marinated salad.
   Place the sliced beef on top of the salad and serve immediately.

Serves 6–8

Couscous with chickpeas, nuts and pomegranate seeds

2 cups couscous
2 red onions, finely chopped
a little olive oil
juice of 1 lemon
lemon peel, cut into thin strips
   using a lemon zester
1 cup chopped fresh flat-leaf parsley
½ cup finely chopped fresh mint
6 spring onions, finely chopped
1 x 400 g tin chickpeas, drained
¼ tsp ground cumin
¼ tsp freshly ground black pepper
sea salt to taste
¼ cup chopped pistachios, toasted
¼ cup flaked almonds, toasted
¼ cup pomegranate arils

1. Cook the couscous according to
   the packet instructions and place
   in a serving bowl.
2. Fry the onions in a little olive oil until
   translucent, and add to the couscous.
3. Gently fold the remaining
   ingredients, except the nuts
   and pomegranate arils, through
   the couscous.
4. Just before serving, fold in
   the pistachios, almonds and
   pomegranate arils.

Serves 6–8

Aromatic chicken curry

2 Tbsp curry mix
a few bay leaves
4–6 cardamom pods
a few mustard seeds
1.5 kg chicken pieces (breasts
 and thighs)
3 Tbsp olive oil
1 onion, chopped
1 clove garlic, chopped
¼ cup chopped fresh ginger
400 ml coconut milk
2 roma tomatoes, quartered
chopped fresh mint and coriander
 leaves for garnishing

1. Grind the curry mix, bay leaves,
   cardamom pods and mustard
   seeds. Rub into the chicken pieces.
2. Heat 1 Tbsp of the olive oil in a
   large saucepan and sauté the onion,
   garlic and ginger until soft. Remove
   from the pan.
3. In the same pan, heat the remaining
   olive oil and brown the chicken.
4. Return the sautéed onions to the
   pan. Add the coconut milk and
   simmer for 10 minutes. Add the
   tomatoes and cook on a low heat
   for about 20 minutes until the
   chicken is cooked through.
5. Garnish with chopped mint
   and coriander, and serve with
   basmati rice.

Serves 6–8

Mediterranean grilled chicken and vegetables

1.5 kg whole chicken
1 onion, peeled and halved
2 cloves garlic, halved
1½ lemons
1 Tbsp chopped fresh thyme
2 tsp chopped fresh parsley
2 tsp chicken spice
sea salt and freshly ground black pepper to taste

1. Preheat the oven to 190 °C.
2. Clean the chicken and trim the fat. Dry well.
3. Place the onion halves in the cavity. Place the garlic in the cavity and under the skin. Peel chunks of skin off 1 lemon and place in the cavity and under the skin. Place the lemon in the cavity too.
4. Squeeze the juice of half a lemon over the chicken. Rub the thyme and parsley over the chicken, placing a little in the cavity. Season with the chicken spice, salt and pepper.
5. Place the chicken in an ovenproof dish and roast for 1 hour until brown and succulent.
6. Cut into portions and serve with the Mediterranean vegetables below.

¼ cup olive oil
5 cloves garlic, halved
200 g fresh mushrooms, halved
1 red onion, cut in chunks
5 roma tomatoes, thickly sliced
1 heaped tsp vegetable stock powder
salt and freshly ground black pepper to taste
120 g mini rosa tomatoes, halved
¾ cup Calamata olives, halved
¼ cup pine nuts, toasted
a handful of cranberries, halved
3 Tbsp chopped fresh parsley

1. Heat the olive oil in a skillet over a high heat and brown the garlic, mushrooms and red onion for approximately 4 minutes.
2. Add the roma tomatoes and stock powder, and fry for approximately 2 minutes. Season to taste.
3. Stir in the rosa tomatoes and olives, and fry for 1 minute. Remove from the heat and spoon next to the chicken on a platter.
4. Top with the pine nuts, cranberries and parsley.

Serves 2–4

Pizza
with cream cheese, smoked salmon and rocket

BASE
1 cup cake flour, sifted
¼ cup olive oil
½ cup milk
1 tsp baking powder
a pinch of salt

TOPPING
½ red onion, thinly sliced
1 Tbsp fresh lemon juice
1 Tbsp olive oil
250 g cream cheese
250 g smoked salmon
100 g rocket
small lemon wedges
freshly ground black pepper to taste
black caviar (optional)

1. Preheat the oven to 180 °C. Grease a round baking tin or rectangular baking tray.
2. Mix the base ingredients to form a dough and press into the baking tin or roll out
   onto the baking tray.
3. Bake for 10–15 minutes until brown and crispy.
4. While the base is baking, marinate the red onion for the topping in the lemon juice and olive oil.
5. When done, remove the pizza base from the tin or tray.
6. Spread the cream cheese over the base and layer the smoked salmon on top.
   Add the rocket and red onion, and scatter over the lemon wedges.
   Season with pepper and add caviar if desired.

Makes 1 large or 2 small pizzas

Sesame-crusted sole
with dill and cucumber sauce

1 large sole per person
fish spice
garlic salt
fresh lemon juice
2 eggs, lightly beaten
cake flour
sesame seeds
sunflower oil

DILL AND CUCUMBER SAUCE
2 Tbsp chopped fresh dill
1 cup chopped English cucumber
⅓ cup chopped spring onion
1 tsp paprika
¼ cup sour cream
1 Tbsp mayonnaise
freshly ground black pepper to taste

1. Wash and dry the soles. Dust with fish spice and garlic salt and squeeze over lemon juice.
2. Dip the soles into the egg to coat, then dip into flour and finally into sesame seeds.
3. Heat a little oil in a large frying pan and fry the soles until cooked.
4. To make the sauce, pulse all the ingredients in a food processor.
5. Serve the fish with the sauce on the side.

Serves 4–6

Buttery boulkas
with sugary streusel

STREUSEL
3 Tbsp cake flour
3 Tbsp sugar
2 Tbsp melted butter

BOULKAS
8 cups cake flour
1 cup sugar
2 tsp salt
250 g butter
1 cup milk
1 cup fresh cream
1 cup warm water
2 x 10 g pkts dry yeast
4 eggs
melted butter
cinnamon sugar

1. First make the streusel by mixing together the flour, sugar and butter until combined. You can store this mixture in a container in the freezer.
2. For the boulkas, sift the flour, sugar and salt into a large bowl.
3. Melt the butter with the milk in a saucepan on the stove. Remove from the heat and add the cream.
4. Place the 1 cup warm water in a separate bowl and sprinkle over the yeast. Do not stir. Cover with clingfilm and allow to stand for 5 minutes until the yeast has proved.
5. Beat the eggs and add to the milk mixture.
6. Make a well in the centre of the dry ingredients and add the yeast. Mix well. Add the milk-egg mixture and knead for 3–5 minutes to make a dough.
7. Cover the bowl with clingfilm and a warm towel and allow to stand until the dough rises (the length of time depends on the room temperature – watch carefully, because dough that rises and stands for too long tends to go sour).
8. Knead the dough again, then re-cover and allow to stand. Repeat this once more, then place on a floured surface and divide into four pieces.
9. Preheat the oven to 190 °C and grease two muffin pans.
10. Roll one piece of dough into a long oval, brush with some melted butter and sprinkle with lots of cinnamon sugar. Roll up and cut into 4 cm-thick rounds. Press the bottom of each round closed, brush the open cut side with more melted butter and sprinkle with streusel. Repeat with the remaining dough.
11. Place the rounds in the muffin pans and bake for approximately 15 minutes until golden.

Makes 24

BRAVE

Pronounced [breyv]

(Adj.) Possessing or displaying valiance, resolution or daring; making a fine display; impressive; having or showing courage under difficult or dangerous conditions, for example frying *fishcakes*. **(Verb tr.)** To challenge; to dare; to defy; to brave the odds; to confront a *cheese soufflé*; to master a *chiffon cake*; to show off your perfect *crème caramel*; to overcome culinary fear; to be a courageous cook; to feel proud. **Synonyms:** Fearless; intrepid; bold; audacious; valorous; mettlesome; plucky; undaunted.

Courageous cheese soufflé

60 g + 1 Tbsp butter
1½ cups coarsely grated cheese, preferably a mixture or just Cheddar
¼ cup cake flour
1¼ cups milk, scalded
1½ tsp salt
⅛ tsp white pepper
⅛ tsp ground mace
⅛ tsp paprika
5 egg yolks, at room temperature
6 egg whites, at room temperature
¼ tsp cream of tartar

1. Preheat the oven to 180 °C. Grease a 1.5-litre soufflé dish with the 1 Tbsp butter. Sprinkle 1 cup grated cheese around the inside of the dish and press into the sides and the bottom. Set aside.
2. In a large saucepan, melt the remaining butter over a medium heat. Stir in the flour and cook, stirring continuously for 1 minute – do not allow this roux to brown.
3. Remove the pan from the heat and gradually stir in the milk. Return to the stove and stir until the mixture becomes thick and smooth.
4. Remove the pan from the heat again and add 1 tsp salt, as well as the pepper, mace and paprika.
5. Beat the egg yolks a little at a time into the hot sauce. Add the remaining cheese and allow the mixture to cool slightly.
6. In a separate bowl, beat the egg whites until foamy. Add the remaining salt and the cream of tartar, and beat until stiff peaks form. Fold the egg whites into the soufflé mixture.
7. Spoon the mixture into the soufflé dish. With a knife, mark a deep circle in the centre.
8. Bake in the middle of the oven for 40–45 minutes or until lightly browned and risen to 1 cm above the top of the dish. Serve immediately.

Serves 4–6

Handmade

Fearless fishcakes

1 kg fresh white fish fillets, such as hake
1 Tbsp fresh lemon juice
1 Tbsp fish spice
2 Tbsp olive oil
2 carrots, peeled and finely grated
1 large onion, chopped
6 spring onions, finely chopped
2 potatoes, peeled, boiled and roughly mashed
½ cup sweet chilli sauce
sea salt and freshly ground black pepper to taste
4 eggs
2 cups cake flour
200 g dried breadcrumbs

1. Preheat the oven to 190 °C. Line a baking tray with greaseproof paper.
2. Sprinkle the fish with the lemon juice and 2 tsp fish spice. Poach the fish in a saucepan of boiling water until just soft. Allow to cool.
3. Heat the olive oil in a pan and sauté the carrots and onion for approximately 5 minutes, until lightly fried.
4. Place the fish, spring onions, carrots and onion, potatoes, remaining fish spice, sweet chilli sauce, salt and pepper in a bowl. Combine well and adjust seasoning.
5. Press the mixture into 6 cm moulds or cups. Remove and place on a lined baking tray. Cover loosely with clingfilm and store in the freezer until frozen.
6. In a separate bowl, beat the eggs. Dip the frozen fishcakes into the flour and shake off the excess. Next, dip them into the beaten egg. Lastly, dip them into the breadcrumbs. Freeze the crumbed fishcakes for at least 4 hours to bind. They can remain frozen until needed.
7. When ready to cook, simply defrost until slightly soft. Heat some oil in a frying pan and fry the fishcakes until golden. They only require browning, as all the ingredients are completely cooked. Serve with a sweet chilli sauce and lemon wedges.

Makes 24

Daring citrus turkey

5 kg turkey
2 oranges, halved
1 onion, peeled
4 cups fresh orange juice
olive oil for brushing
1 Tbsp cornflour

TURKEY RUB
2 tsp paprika
3 heaped Tbsp chicken stock powder
2 tsp white pepper
2 tsp sea salt
2 Tbsp ground ginger or crushed fresh ginger
2 Tbsp sunflower oil

1. Preheat the oven to 200 °C.
2. Clean the turkey well and place in a greased roasting pan.
3. Make the rub by combining all the ingredients. Dip 2 orange halves in the rub and use to dab the turkey all over, inside and out, until well coated.
4. Place the onion and the remaining 2 orange halves inside the turkey and pour over the orange juice. Tie the drumsticks and wings with string.
5. Brush the turkey with oil, cover with foil, shiny-side facing inwards, and roast for 1 hour.
6. Remove, uncover and turn down the oven to 180 °C. Place the turkey back in the oven and brown for 1 hour, basting every 20 minutes. Check the leg to see if the turkey is cooked.
7. When cooked, remove the turkey from the pan. Pour the remaining pan juices into a saucepan. Allow to cool slightly and skim off the excess fat. Add the cornflour and heat the mixture until it thickens slightly, forming a gravy.
8. Carve the turkey, place the meat in a casserole dish and cover with the gravy.

Serves 10–12

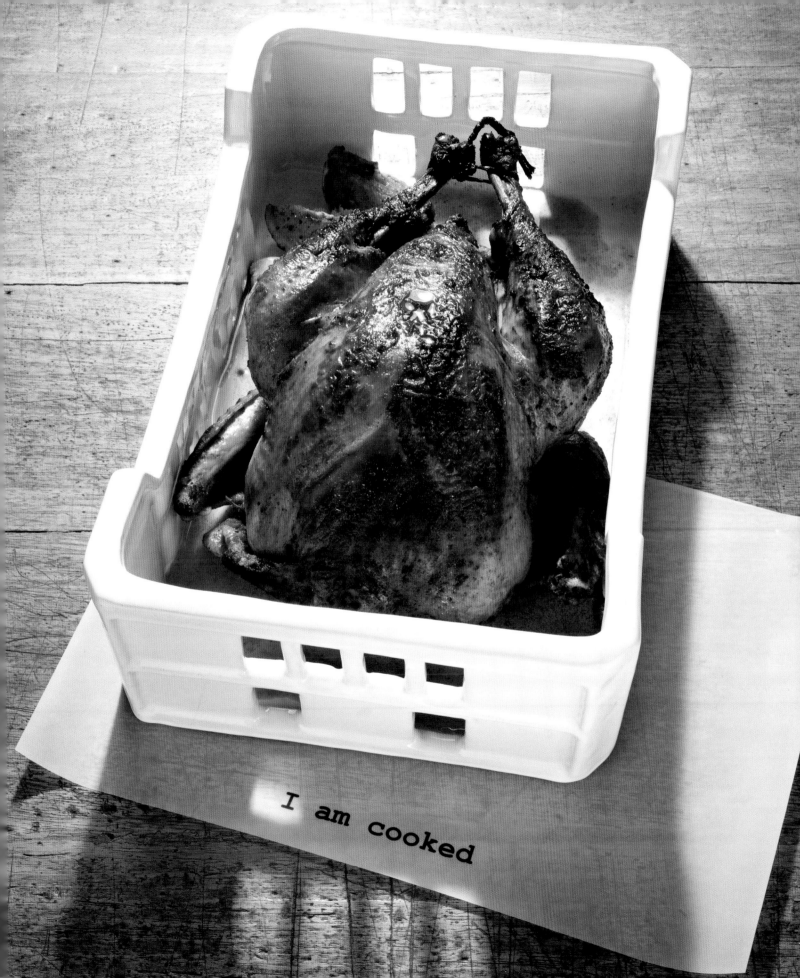

I am cooked

I won't flop chiffon cake

2 level cups cake flour
1 cup sugar
a pinch of salt
3 tsp baking powder
1 Tbsp custard powder
2 Tbsp cornflour
½ cup oil
¾ cup boiling water
6 jumbo eggs, separated,
    at room temperature
icing sugar for dusting

1. Preheat the oven to 180 °C.
2. Sift the flour, sugar, salt, 2 tsp of the baking powder, custard powder and cornflour together. Make a well in the centre and add the oil, boiling water and egg yolks. Beat for 5 minutes with an electric beater on a medium speed.
3. In a separate bowl, beat the egg whites until frothy. Add the remaining baking powder and continue to beat on a high speed until stiff. Gently fold the yolk mixture into the egg whites.
4. Pour the mixture into an ungreased chiffon tin and bake on the middle shelf of the oven for 35 minutes. Turn off the oven, leaving the cake in for 5 minutes.
5. Invert the tin over the neck of a bottle and allow to cool completely. When cold, remove the cake from the tin with a metal spatula or long sharp knife and dust with icing sugar.
6. Serve with warmed homemade marmelade (see page 39) mixed with 1 Tbsp brandy.

Valorous chocolate mousse

2 Tbsp cocoa powder
250 g good-quality chocolate
8 egg yolks, at room temperature
½ cup sugar
3 Tbsp chocolate liqueur
1 cup fresh cream
6 egg whites
your favourite decadent chocolate,
    crumbled, for decorating

1. Dissolve the cocoa powder in the
   chocolate in a double boiler
   (make sure the water does not boil
   too fast). Spray a wooden spoon
   with non-stick cooking spray before
   mixing. Remove from the heat.
2. Beat the egg yolks with the sugar,
   and add to the chocolate mixture.
   Whisk in the liqueur.
3. Whip the cream until just fluffy
   (be careful not to over beat, as it
   will collapse), and then fold into
   the mixture.
4. Beat the egg whites until stiff and
   fold into the mixture.
5. Sprinkle the top with your favourite
   decadent chocolate and place in the
   fridge until ready to serve.

(To make a white chocolate mousse,
use white chocolate and do
not add cocoa powder.)

Serves 6–8

Handcrafted crème caramel

CARAMEL

2 cups sugar

¼ cup water

CUSTARD BASE

2 x 380 g tins Ideal milk

1 tsp vanilla essence

1½ cups sugar

12 egg yolks, at room temperature

1. To make the caramel, boil the sugar with the water in a saucepan over a medium heat. Shake the pan, do not stir. Rather tilt the pan to swirl the mixture. When the sugar dissolves and starts to turn a light caramel colour, remove from the stove. (Please be careful, caramel burns quickly.)
2. Pour the caramel into individual 7 cm-diameter ramekins or rectangular ovenproof dishes. Tilt the dishes to distribute the caramel evenly over the base.
3. Preheat the oven to 200 °C.
4. To make the custard, pour the Ideal milk, vanilla essence and sugar into a saucepan. Stir over a medium heat until small bubbles appear, and then remove from the heat.
5. Whisk the egg yolks until pale and creamy. Slowly add the hot cream mixture to the egg yolks, whisking continuously until combined.
6. Using a fine sieve, strain the mixture into a jug.
7. Line a roasting pan with cloths or a tea towel. Place the caramel-lined dishes onto the cloth. Pour in the custard. Pour boiling water into the roasting pan until half-full.
8. Bake for 45 minutes, then reduce the temperature to 120 °C and bake for a further 15 minutes. Turn off the oven, but leave the crème caramel in for 30 minutes.
9. Remove from the oven, allow to cool and place in the fridge until ready to serve.

Serves 6–8

This dish does not contain professionally procured assistance. 100% naturally handcrafted.

Easy-peasy pavlova

6 egg whites, at room temperature
1½ cups castor sugar
1 Tbsp cornflour
2 tsp white vinegar
½ tsp vanilla essence
a pinch of salt

1. Preheat the oven to 150 °C. Line a large baking tray with baking paper.
2. Beat the egg whites until peaks form. Continue beating, gradually adding the castor sugar until it dissolves and the mixture appears thick and silky.
3. Add the cornflour, vinegar, vanilla essence and salt, all while beating.
4. Spoon the mixture onto the baking paper in a circular shape.
5. Bake for 10 minutes, then reduce the temperature to 110 °C and bake for 1 hour. The pavlova should be crispy and dry.
6. Turn off the oven, but leave the pavlova in until completely cool.
7. Serve with mascarpone cheese, fresh berries and berry coulis (see page 61) or the granadilla topping below.

GRANADILLA TOPPING
1 cup sour cream
100 g icing sugar, sifted
pulp of 1 granadilla
200 g fresh gooseberries for decorating

1. Mix the sour cream, sugar and granadilla pulp.
2. Smooth over the pavlova and top with the fresh gooseberries.

Serves 6–8

VINTAGE

Pronounced [vin-tij]
(Adj.) Belonging to the highest rank or class; serving as the established model or standard; a *classic cheesecake*; having lasting significance or worth; enduring; my great grandmother's recipe for *brandy tart*; of a well-known type; typical; elegant; a traditional example of *macaroni cheese*; characterised by balance, regularity and purity of form; recipes entangled in childhood memories; always a hot favourite because of its simplicity; much loved memorable 'basics'.

Avocado ritz

2 kg firm white fish, skinned and filleted
a few bay leaves and peppercorns
4 avocados
mixed salad leaves
fresh lemon juice
freshly ground black pepper
paprika
grated rind of 2 lemons

SAUCE
2 cups mayonnaise
1 cup tomato sauce
1 Tbsp fresh lemon juice
1 Tbsp brandy
Tabasco® sauce to taste
salt and freshly ground black pepper to taste

1. Poach the fish with the bay leaves and peppercorns in salted water, until just cooked.
   The fish must not be too soft. Remove from the water, drain, cool and place in the fridge.
2. Make the sauce by combining all the ingredients and mixing well. Adjust seasoning
   and chill in the fridge.
3. A few hours before serving, cut the fish into big chunks. Fold in the chilled sauce.
4. Slice the avocados into chunks and arrange in the bottom of glass cocktail dishes
   (1 per person). Add a few salad leaves, squeeze lemon juice over and season with
   black pepper.
5. Spoon the fish on top and sprinkle with paprika and more black pepper.
   Garnish with grated lemon rind.

Serves 6–8

Macaroni cheese

500 g macaroni
a little olive oil
125 g butter
3 Tbsp cake flour
2 cups grated mature Cheddar cheese
2½–3 cups milk
2 tsp Dijon mustard
1 tsp paprika
sea salt and freshly ground black pepper to taste
½ cup grated Parmesan cheese
1 x 125 g pkt salt and vinegar crisps or any spicy crisps, crushed

1. Preheat the oven to 180 °C.
2. Cook the macaroni in a pot of salted water. Drain and toss with a little olive oil to prevent sticking. Set aside.
3. Melt the butter over a low heat. Add the flour, Cheddar, milk, mustard and paprika. Stir until thick, combined and smooth. Season with salt and pepper.
4. Combine the pasta and cheese sauce and transfer to a roughly 37 x 18 cm ovenproof dish. Sprinkle over the Parmesan and crisps.
5. Bake for about 25 minutes until hot. The topping should be golden and crispy.
6. Remove from the oven and allow to stand for 5–7 minutes before serving.

Serves 6–8

Bolognese

2 Tbsp olive oil
2 onions, finely chopped
1 clove garlic, crushed
1.5 kg steak mince
2 x 425 g tins chopped tomatoes
1 Tbsp tomato paste
1 tsp peri-peri tomato sauce
1 Tbsp brown onion soup powder
½ cup water
1 tsp dried basil
1 tsp dried origanum
1 tsp chopped fresh parsley
salt and freshly ground black pepper to taste
500 g spaghetti or any pasta of your choice

1. Heat the oil in a frying pan and sauté the onions and garlic until soft.
2. Add the mince and brown. Stir with a fork to break up any clumps.
3. Add the tomatoes with their juice, the tomato paste, peri-peri tomato sauce, soup powder, water, basil, origanum, parsley, salt and pepper. Mix well.
4. Simmer, uncovered, for approximately 1½ hours until the liquid reduces to a sauce – not too watery or too thick.
5. Cook the pasta according to the packet instructions. Drain and combine with the sauce in a large serving bowl.

Serves 6–8

Rustic rosti cottage pie

Make a batch of bolognese as described in the bolognese recipe on page 280 and then commence with the recipe below.

500 g butternut, peeled and cut into small chunks
6 baby marrows, cut into chunks
4 sweet potatoes, peeled and cut into chunks
a little olive oil
vegetable seasoning
3 large potatoes, peeled

1. Preheat the oven to 180 °C. Spray a baking tray with non-stick cooking spray.
2. Place the butternut, baby marrows and sweet potatoes on the tray, drizzle over a little olive oil and sprinkle with vegetable seasoning, and toss. Roast for about 20 minutes until tender.
3. Add the vegetables to the bolognese and transfer to an ovenproof dish.
4. Parboil the potatoes. Cool for a few minutes and then grate.
5. Spoon the grated potato on top of the mince and spread it out.
6. Brush with olive oil and bake for about 20 minutes until crispy and browned.

Serves 6–8

Caramel treat

a pinch of salt

1 x 360 g tin caramel treat or 1 x 385 g tin condensed milk, boiled until it becomes caramel

6 meringues, roughly crushed or left whole

1 litre vanilla ice cream

100 g honeycomb chocolate or Cadbury Crunchie™, roughly chopped

1. Add the salt to the caramel treat or boiled condensed milk.
2. For individual servings, place 1 Tbsp caramel into each parfait glass.
3. Place a layer of meringue on top, add a scoop of ice cream and top with the chopped chocolate. Repeat the layers if the glass is large enough.

Serves 6–8

Fruity trifle

1 small Madeira cake or 8 mini
  Swiss rolls
2 cups granadilla juice
½ cup Amarula Cream
1½ cups fresh cream, beaten
350 ml vanilla yoghurt
1 large mango, peeled and chopped
1 large nectarine, peeled and chopped
1 small pineapple, peeled and chopped
2 kiwi fruits, peeled and chopped
a few strawberries, halved
1 cup coarsely chopped cashew
  nut brittle

1. Slice the cake or Swiss rolls into
   1 cm-thick slices. Cut each slice
   in half. Soak the sliced cake in
   the granadilla juice for a few
   minutes (do not allow the cake
   to become soggy).
2. Fold the Amarula Cream into
   the cream.
3. Place a layer of cake in a pie dish or
   glass serving bowl and spoon over
   half of the yoghurt.
4. Spoon over half of the cream
   mixture.
5. Scatter over half of the chopped
   fruit and repeat the layers. Top with
   the chopped nut brittle, cover and
   refrigerate overnight.

Serves 6–8

Cheesecake

125 g butter or margarine, softened
1 x 200 g pkt Marie or tea biscuits, crushed
2 Tbsp sugar

FILLING
4 x 250 g tubs smooth cream cheese
2 heaped Tbsp cake flour
1 cup sugar
1 cup thick fresh cream
4 eggs
1 Tbsp fresh lemon juice
1 Tbsp brandy or whiskey
1 tsp vanilla essence

TOPPING
1 cup sour cream
3 Tbsp castor sugar
1 drop vanilla essence

1. Preheat the oven to 170 °C.
2. Melt the butter or margarine in a saucepan, add the biscuits and sugar, and mix.
3. Press into a springform cake tin or large ovenproof dish.
4. At a slow speed, beat the cream cheese, flour, sugar and cream.
5. Add the eggs, one at a time, beating slowly.
6. Add the lemon juice, brandy or whiskey and vanilla essence, and mix.
   Pour over the biscuit base.
7. Bake for 30 minutes and then switch off the oven for 5 minutes. Open the oven door slightly and leave the cheesecake in for 30 minutes. Remove from the oven, allow to cool and refrigerate overnight.
8. Mix the topping ingredients and pour over the chilled cheesecake. Allow to set for 1 hour before serving. Decorate as desired.

For a more adventurous topping, mix passion fruit curd (see page 105) with the sour cream topping mixture.

Serves 6–8

Mini brandy tart loaves

2 Tbsp butter, softened
¾ cup sugar
1 jumbo egg, at room temperature
1 cup fresh dates, pitted and chopped
1 tsp bicarbonate of soda
1 cup boiling water
1¼ cups cake flour
a pinch of salt
½ tsp baking powder
¼ cup chopped pecans
icing sugar for dusting
whipped cream for serving

SYRUP
1 cup sugar
¾ cup water
1 Tbsp butter
½ cup brandy
1 tsp vanilla essence

1. Preheat the oven to 180 °C. Grease 10 mini loaf tins (8 x 5 x 3 cm high).
2. Cream the butter and sugar, add the egg, and set aside.
3. Place the dates in a separate bowl and sprinkle over the bicarbonate of soda. Add the boiling water.
4. Sift the flour, salt and baking powder together in a large mixing bowl.
5. Add the butter and date mixtures alternately to the flour. Stir in the nuts.
6. Pour the batter into the loaf tins and bake for 20 minutes. Allow to cool before removing from the tins.
7. In the meantime, make the syrup. Boil the sugar, water, butter, brandy and vanilla essence for 5 minutes in a saucepan. Allow to cool before pouring over the loaves. Dust with icing sugar and serve with cream.

Makes 10 mini loaves

Chocolaty bread and butter pudding

6–8 croissants, cut in half lengthways
    through the middle
200 g Nutella® or any praline
    chocolate spread
4 eggs
½ cup sugar
1 cup water
a pinch of salt
2 cups fresh cream
1 Tbsp ground cinnamon
80 g good-quality chocolate, grated

1. Preheat the oven to 180 °C.
   Grease a 28 x 15 cm pie dish.
2. Lightly toast the croissants and
   spread with the Nutella®.
3. Arrange the croissants upright
   in the dish (do not lie them flat).
4. Beat the eggs with the sugar and
   water. Add the salt.
5. Lightly beat the cream and
   fold into the egg mixture. Spoon
   the mixture over the croissants.
6. Sprinkle with the cinnamon and
   top with the grated chocolate.
7. Bake for 50–60 minutes until the
   custard has set, but is still moist.
   This is delicious served with
   chocolate sauce, such as the chunky
   rocky road fudge sauce on page 63.

Serves 6–8

Crêpes suzette

1½ cups cake flour
2 tsp sugar
a pinch of salt
3 eggs
3 cups milk
1 tsp vanilla essence
¼ cup melted butter, cooled
a little butter for cooking

FILLING
250 g butter, softened
2 Tbsp soft brown sugar
1 Tbsp Grand Marnier
½ tsp vanilla essence
⅔ cup ground almonds

SAUCE
2 cups orange juice
¼ cup brandy
grated orange rind for sprinkling

1. Sift the flour, sugar and salt into a mixing bowl. Make a well in the centre and add the eggs, one at a time. Beat until blended.
2. Gradually pour in the milk and vanilla essence, beating well after each addition until the mixture forms a smooth batter. Stir in the cooled butter. Allow the mixture to rest for a few hours.
3. Heat a little butter in a small frying pan. When sizzling, pour in a little batter and tilt the pan to cover the base. Cook over a medium heat until the crêpe is light brown underneath. Turn over and cook for another minute. Repeat for the remaining batter.
4. To make the filling, cream the butter and sugar. Add the Grand Marnier and vanilla essence, and mix well. Fold in the almonds.
5. Spread a layer of filling over each crêpe. Fold the crêpe in half and then in half again to form a quarter. Repeat for the remaining crêpes.
6. Preheat the oven to 180 °C. Grease an ovenproof dish. Place the crêpes in the dish, slightly overlapping.
7. For the sauce, boil the orange juice and brandy for 3–4 minutes in a small saucepan. Pour over the crêpes and top with the orange rind.
8. Cover and bake for 15 minutes.

Serves 6–8

NURTURE

Pronounced [nur-cher]
(Noun) Something that nourishes; sustenance; fine ingredients treated simply; earthy flavours; pots of goodness. **(Verb tr.)** To help grow or develop; to cultivate; to feed and protect; to support and encourage; to feed one nutritionally; to boost with simple, sumptuous, *seasonal dishes*.

Warm sautéed green vegetables

150 g fine French beans
100 g mangetout
100 g shelled peas
100 g edamame
¼ cup olive oil
2 tsp crushed garlic
6 shallots, chopped
¼ cup chopped fresh mint
sea salt and freshly ground black pepper to taste
1 Tbsp vegetable spice
½ cup slivered almonds, toasted

1. Boil the beans in salted water for 3 minutes. Drain and submerge in cold water.
2. Repeat for the mangetout, peas and edamame.
3. Heat the olive oil in a frying pan. Add the garlic and shallots, and sauté until soft.
4. Add the mint and mix.
5. Add the beans, mangetout, peas and edamame.
6. Season with salt, pepper and vegetable spice.
7. Scatter over the almonds and serve.

Serves 4–6

Spicy lentils

500 g lentils
salt and freshly ground black pepper to taste
125 g salted butter
a drop of olive oil
1 onion, chopped
1 tsp chopped fresh chilli
1 tsp chopped garlic
1 tsp chopped fresh ginger
½ cup water
1 cup white wine
½ cup sweet chilli sauce
1 tsp ground cumin
2 tsp balsamic vinegar
2 tsp soy sauce
1 cup chopped fresh coriander
¼ cup chopped spring onion
½ red pepper, deseeded and chopped

1. Boil the lentils according to the packet instructions until almost cooked. Season with salt and pepper.
2. In a separate saucepan, melt the butter and a drop of olive oil. Add the onion and sauté until soft, then add the chilli, garlic and ginger.
3. Add the lentils to the pan, followed by the water, wine, sweet chilli sauce, cumin, balsamic vinegar and soy sauce. Stir.
4. Add the coriander and simmer for 10–15 minutes. Taste and adjust the seasoning.
5. Transfer to a serving bowl and garnish with the chopped spring onion and red pepper.

Serves 6–8

Fusion tofu stir-fry

1 tsp grated fresh ginger
2 tsp chopped garlic
1 red onion, thinly sliced
2 fresh red chillies, deseeded and chopped
¼ cup olive oil
2 shallots, sliced lengthways
6 spring onions, finely sliced
4 leeks, finely sliced
200 g tofu, dried and cubed
½ cup cake flour
2 Tbsp olive oil
2 Tbsp soy sauce
2 Tbsp sugar
2 tsp sesame oil
100 g bean sprouts
150 g baby spinach, coarsely chopped

1. Mix the ginger, garlic, onion and chillies.
2. Heat the ¼ cup olive oil in a wok over a medium heat and sauté the garlic mixture for 2 minutes.
3. Add the shallots, spring onions and leeks, and cook for a further 2 minutes.
4. Coat the tofu in the flour and set aside.
5. Remove the garlic mixture from the wok and set aside.
6. Add the 2 Tbsp olive oil, the soy sauce, sugar and sesame oil to the wok, followed by the tofu.
7. Fry the tofu for a few minutes before stirring in the garlic mixture and bean sprouts. Cook for 1 minute.
8. Remove from the heat and fold in the baby spinach. Serve immediately.

Serves 4–6

Honey–Ginger sweet potato bake

2 Tbsp grated fresh ginger
3 Tbsp honey
juice of 1 lemon
2 Tbsp onion stock powder
¼ cup olive oil
6 sweet potatoes, washed and
   thickly sliced (do not peel)

1. Preheat the oven to 200 °C.
2. Mix the ginger, honey, lemon juice,
   onion powder and olive oil and rub
   into the sweet potatoes.
3. Layer the potatoes in an
   ovenproof dish.
4. Bake until the sweet potatoes are
   soft and browned, about 40 minutes.

Serves 4–6

Mini vegetable bakes

4 medium baby marrows
4 large carrots, peeled
1 onion
2 potatoes, peeled
4 eggs
⅔ cup vegetable oil
6 Tbsp seasoned dried breadcrumbs
1 tsp salt
1 tsp vegetable stock powder
½ tsp freshly ground black pepper
1 tsp paprika
sprigs of fresh rosemary for garnishing

1. Preheat the oven to 180 °C. Grease a
   25 cm-square ovenproof baking dish
   or line a muffin pan, placing squares
   of greaseproof paper in each cup.
2. Finely grate all the vegetables
   into a bowl.
3. In a separate bowl, beat the eggs.
   Add the oil, breadcrumbs, salt, stock
   powder, black pepper and paprika,
   and pour over the grated vegetables.
4. Mix well and spoon into the
   baking dish or muffin pan.
5. Bake for approximately 1 hour until
   crispy. Garnish with fresh rosemary.

Serves 4–6

Pumpkin wedges
with honey and nuts

1 kg pumpkin, peeled, deseeded
    and cut into 3 cm wedges
a little olive oil
vegetable seasoning to taste
sea salt and freshly ground
    black pepper to taste
120 g butter, softened
¼ cup honey
200 g raw cashews, chopped

1. Preheat the oven to 180 °C and
    grease a baking tray with a little
    olive oil.
2. Toss the pumpkin wedges in a little
    olive oil to coat and season with
    vegetable seasoning,
    sea salt and black pepper.
3. Place the wedges on the baking tray
    and bake for about 25 minutes until
    the pumpkin is almost soft. Remove
    from the oven and lie the wedges
    flat on the tray.
4. Combine the butter, honey and
    chopped cashews and spread this
    mixture over the pumpkin.
5. Bake for a further 15–20 minutes
    until the pumpkin is cooked and the
    topping becomes brown.

Serves 4–6

Crispy Parmesan-coated cauliflower

400 g cauliflower florets
2 cloves garlic,
finely chopped
1 Tbsp vegetable seasoning
a little olive oil
1 Tbsp melted butter
½ cup dried breadcrumbs
¼ cup finely grated Parmesan cheese
freshly ground black pepper to taste

1. Preheat the oven to 200 °C.
   Grease a baking tray.
2. Wash and dry the cauliflower
   and place on the baking sheet.
   Sprinkle over the garlic and
   vegetable seasoning, and toss
   with a little olive oil.
3. Bake for 10–15 minutes until
   the cauliflower is almost soft.
4. Mix the butter, breadcrumbs
   and Parmesan, and spoon over
   the cauliflower.
5. Return to the oven and cook for
   10–12 minutes until golden.
6. Season with black pepper and serve.

Serves 4

Rosemary potatoes

1.5 kg potatoes (do not peel)
¼ cup olive oil
8 sprigs fresh rosemary, snipped
sea salt and freshly ground black pepper to taste

1. Preheat the oven to 180 °C. Grease an ovenproof dish.
2. Boil the potatoes in salted water for 10–15 minutes. Drain and pat dry.
3. Place the potatoes in the greased dish, gently pressing them with your hand. Spoon over the olive oil and season with the rosemary, salt and pepper.
4. Roast in the oven for 45–60 minutes, depending on the size of the potatoes, until they are golden and crispy. Serve immediately.

Serves 6–8

Jewelled basmati rice

2 cups basmati rice
50 g butter
½ tsp ground pink peppercorns
½ tsp seasoned sea salt
½ cup dried cranberries
½ cup chopped dried apricots
½ cup coarsely chopped pistachios
½ cup pumpkin seeds

1. Boil the rice according to the packet instructions until almost ready.
2. Melt the butter in a large saucepan, add the rice and toss.
   Season with the pink peppercorns and sea salt.
3. Add the cranberries and apricots, and stir until combined.
4. Stir in the pistachios and pumpkin seeds and serve.

Serves 4–6

Baked potato wedges
with sweet chilli dipping sauce

7 potatoes, cut in half and each half cut into 3 wedges (do not peel)
2 Tbsp olive oil
1 tsp garlic flakes
1 Tbsp sea salt

1. Preheat the oven to 180 °C. Lightly grease a baking tray.
2. Toss the wedges with the olive oil, garlic flakes and sea salt.
3. Place on the tray and bake for about 1¼ hours until brown and crispy.
4. Serve immediately with the dipping sauce below.

SWEET CHILLI DIPPING SAUCE
1 x 400 g tin Italian tomatoes
1 tsp sea salt
1 tsp garlic flakes
¼ cup balsamic vinegar
¼ cup brown sugar
¼ cup chopped fresh coriander
3 fresh red chillies, chopped

1. Place all the ingredients in a saucepan and heat, stirring continuously until the sugar dissolves. Simmer, uncovered, until the mixture thickens.
2. Remove from the heat and cool slightly.
3. Blend in a food processor until smooth and serve with the potato wedges.

Serves 4–6

MESS

Pronounced [mes]
(Noun) A quantity of food; a prepared dish of soft food; a mixture of ingredients cooked or eaten together. **(Verb tr.)** To be sticky; to be silly and sugared-up. **Synonyms:** Chance-medley; confusion; disarrangement; dishevelment; disorder; jumble; shambles; *mash muddle; disarrayed jelly cake; icky sticky yummy recipes for the child in everyone.* **Tip:** Serve with serviettes, wipes, and soap and water.

Make your own
mini pizzas

mini-pizza bases (use the recipe
    on page 253, making mini
    bases, or buy ready-made
    mini-pizza bases)
tomato paste

**PLACE THE FOLLOWING
    IN SEPARATE BOWLS**
grated mozzarella cheese
grated Cheddar cheese
sliced tomatoes
pitted olives

1. Preheat the oven to 180 °C.
2. Spread the bases with tomato
    paste and let kids make their
    own mini pizzas, using the
    variety of toppings on offer.
3. Bake until brown and crispy,
    about 5–7 minutes.

Fried **fish fingers** and potato sticks

1 kg firm white fish,
  cut into fingers
fish spice
cake flour
1 egg, lightly beaten
sunflower oil for frying

1. Wash and dry the fish.
   Season with fish spice, coat in
   flour and then dip in the egg.
2. Heat the oil in a frying pan
   and fry the fish until golden.
3. Serve with the following
   potato sticks.

POTATO STICKS

4 potatoes, peeled and sliced
  into matchsticks
sunflower oil for frying
salt and vinegar for serving

1. Fry the potatoes in shallow
   oil until golden. Drain on
   paper towels and toss with
   salt and vinegar.
2. Serve with the fish fingers
   and tomato sauce.

Serves 6–8

Fun mish-mash

300 g fluffy, medium, white potatoes, peeled

25 ml fresh cream

1 Tbsp olive oil

1 Tbsp grated Gouda or Emmenthal cheese

a pinch of Herbamare® organic herb seasoning salt

1. Boil the potatoes for 30 minutes. Dry and mash in a bowl. While warm, add the remaining ingredients.
2. Mash until the mixture is completely smooth; use a potato ricer if you have one.
3. Place the mash in a piping bag and make pictures or shapes using the mash. For example, clouds or steam from a train.

Serves 4–6

Put it together **pasta**

1 x 250 g pkt kiddies pasta
1 tsp olive oil

1. Boil the pasta with the olive oil to prevent sticking. Drain and rinse under cold water.
2. Serve with a selection of the following in little bowls or on a plate, for kids to choose: Napoletana sauce (see page 99); grated cheese; chopped fresh herbs; cheese sauce.

Serves 4–6

Super sticky **chicken drumsticks**

2–3 chicken drumsticks per child

Herbamare® organic herb seasoning salt to taste

a pinch of white pepper

½ cup Worcestershire sauce

½ cup tomato sauce

2 Tbsp honey

2 Tbsp brown sugar

2 Tbsp apricot jam

1 Tbsp olive oil

2 Tbsp vinegar

1. Wash the drumsticks and pat dry. Season with the seasoning salt and white pepper.
2. Mix the remaining ingredients in a flat-bottomed dish.
3. Toss the drumsticks in the sauce, cover and marinate overnight.
4. When ready to cook, preheat the oven to 200 °C.
5. Bake, uncovered, until cooked (30–40 minutes depending on the size of the drumsticks), basting and turning the drumsticks occasionally. Alternatively, cook on the barbecue.

Open **sandwich rainbow platter**

a loaf of sliced bread or round crackers

PLACE THE FOLLOWING IN SEPARATE BOWLS
grated cheese, cream cheese, cottage cheese, chopped tomato,
   sliced cucumber, halved olives, egg mayonnaise, tuna mayonnaise,
   smoked salmon ribbons, sliced banana, fresh strawberries,
   peanut butter, Nutella®

1. Using a cookie cutter, cut the bread into rounds.
2. Allow the kids to place toppings of their choice on the
   bread rounds or crackers and position them on a platter
   in circles or in rows.

Frozen fruit **ice pops**

1 cup fresh fruit, such as strawberries,
  granadilla pulp, pineapple, mixed
  berries, kiwi, mango, banana,
  pomegranate, apple
4 cups vanilla yoghurt or 1 cup iced tea
8 plastic ice-lolly moulds
8 ice-lolly sticks

1. Blend each fruit separately in a food
   processor until smooth.
2. Combine each fruit purée with the
   yoghurt or iced tea in a bowl.
3. Spoon into the moulds – add fresh
   sliced fruit if desired – and place
   in the freezer.
4. When slightly frozen, place an
   ice-lolly stick in the centre and
   freeze until well frozen.

Optional lolly combinations:
blackberry and yoghurt; raspberry and
yoghurt; blueberry and yoghurt; mango
and yoghurt; guava and granadilla;
strawberry; granadilla purée with pips;
strawberry and kiwi; orange juice and
banana; pineapple and banana; apple
iced tea and pomegranate

Makes 8

Layered jelly cake

a range of different jellies

rectangular perspex or Lucite™ stackable boxes
  (available from home depot stores)

chopped fresh fruit and berries for garnishing

1. Make the jellies in the stackable boxes according to the packet instructions. Allow to set in the fridge.
2. When set, garnish each layer with chopped fresh fruit.
3. Assemble the boxes, stacking one on top of the other. If there's a birthday, place birthday candles in the top layer.
4. Separate the boxes and serve with spoons.

Sinful **sundaes**

500 g strawberries, hulled

½ cup water

2 Tbsp icing sugar

1 x 1-litre tub vanilla ice cream

4 chocolate bars, roughly chopped

1 cup unsalted chopped nuts

½ cup chopped glacé cherries

CHOCOLATE SAUCE

4 Mars Bar chocolate bars

¼ cup fresh cream

1. Macerate the strawberries with the water and icing sugar.
2. Scoop the ice cream into bowls or sundae glasses.
3. Spoon over the strawberries and sprinkle with the chopped chocolate.
4. Melt the Mars bars and cream in a double boiler.
5. Drizzle the chocolate sauce over the ice cream and top with the nuts and cherries.
6. Alternatively, serve the strawberries separately with a variety of other toppings for the kids to choose from – M&M's®, 100's and 1000's, crumbled Cadbury Flake®, mini marshmallows, etc.

Serves 10

Colourful **cupcake sarmie**

1 vanilla sponge loaf, approximately 22 x 12 x 6 cm

125 g butter, softened

2 cups icing sugar

a little milk to make the right consistency

a few drops of food colouring

jelly tots, jelly beans, strands of short liquorice,
  liquorice allsorts, chunks of chocolate, Smarties
  or M&M's®, 100's and 1000's, etc. for topping

1. Slice the cake lengthways horizontally to make three layers.
2. Mix the butter and icing sugar, adding a little milk to achieve a spreadable consistency.
3. Divide the icing into three batches and add a different food colouring to each.
4. Spread the bottom layer of cake with one icing, position the middle layer on top and ice this with a different colour.
5. Replace the top layer of cake and ice with the final batch of icing.
6. Decorate with your toppings of choice.

Serves 6

BAKE

Pronounced [beyk]

(Verb) To cook and make edible by putting in a hot oven; the technique of prolonged cooking of food by dry heat acting by convection, normally in an oven. Somewhat scientific precision infused with a dash of art and an irrepressible love for a homey aroma. **(Noun plural)** *Cakes, pastries, pies, tarts, quiches, biscuits, cookies, muffins, scones, etc.* Incorporating chocolate, fruit, nuts and extracts, and sometimes covered with rich creamy frosting or a glaze – *the cherry on the top*. Recipes for bliss; sinful indulgence; a taste of heaven. Practice makes a baker. **Tip:** Lick the bowl.

Caramel macadamia cupcakes

125 g butter
1 cup sugar
3 eggs, at room temperature
1¾ cups cake flour
2 tsp baking powder
a pinch of salt
½ cup milk
½ tsp vanilla essence
100 g Wilson's Cream Caramels (or any cream caramels) + a few extra for decorating
¾ cup roughly chopped macadamia nuts, toasted

ICING
3 Tbsp boiling water
1 Tbsp treacle sugar
1 Tbsp golden syrup
½ tsp vanilla essence
2 cups icing sugar, sifted

1. Preheat the oven to 180 °C. Grease a muffin pan and line with paper casings.
2. Cream the butter and sugar in a large mixing bowl.
3. Add the eggs, one at a time, and beat until the mixture appears white.
4. Sift the flour, baking powder and salt and add to the mixture, alternating with the milk.
5. Add the vanilla essence, cream caramels and nuts and beat for 1 minute until well mixed.
6. Spoon the mixture into the muffin pan (each cup should be three-quarters full) and bake for 15–20 minutes. Allow to cool while you make the icing.
7. Heat the water and treacle sugar in a saucepan over a low heat until the sugar dissolves.
8. Add the syrup and vanilla essence. Add the icing sugar, slowly mixing all the time. If the mixture becomes too thick, add a little more boiling water.
9. Allow to cool slightly before spreading over the tops of the cooled cupcakes.
10. Decorate with cream caramel bits before the icing sets.

Makes 6 giant or 12 regular cupcakes

Beetroot muffins
with creamy lime frosting

1 cup sugar

1½ cups sunflower oil

4 large eggs, at room temperature

2 cups cake flour

2 tsp bicarbonate of soda

2 tsp baking powder

1 tsp ground cinnamon

½ tsp ground nutmeg

1 tsp salt

3 cups grated raw beetroot + a little extra for decorating

1 cup chopped pecans

¼ cup dried cranberries

FROSTING

2 cups icing sugar

250 g cream cheese

zest of ½ lime

juice of ½ lime

½ cup butter, at room temperature

1. Preheat the oven to 180 °C. Grease a muffin pan and line with paper casings.
2. Beat the sugar and oil. Add the eggs, one at a time, beating well after each addition.
3. In a separate bowl, sift together the flour, bicarbonate of soda, baking powder, cinnamon, nutmeg and salt. Add this to the oil mixture.
4. Stir in the beetroot, pecans and cranberries.
5. Pour into the muffin pan and bake for 30–40 minutes.
6. Remove the muffins from the pan and allow to cool.
7. To make the frosting, blend all the ingredients until smooth. Spread over the cooled muffins.
8. Decorate with extra grated beetroot.

Makes 12

Banana and carrot cake
with cinnamon–cream cheese frosting

1 cup sugar
½ cup treacle sugar
4 eggs, at room temperature
1 cup vegetable oil
2 cups cake flour
¼ tsp salt
2 tsp ground cinnamon
2 tsp bicarbonate of soda
1½ cups finely grated carrot
1 cup crushed tinned pineapple
1 cup mashed banana
¾ cup chopped pecans

FROSTING
2 cups icing sugar
250 g cream cheese
½ cup butter, at room temperature
4 tsp vanilla essence
½ tsp ground cinnamon
banana chips for decorating

1. Preheat the oven to 180 °C and grease a 24 cm bundt tin.
2. Beat the sugar, treacle sugar, eggs and oil. Sift in the flour, salt, cinnamon and bicarbonate of soda. Fold in the carrot, pineapple, banana and pecans.
3. Pour the mixture into the tin and bake for 50–55 minutes. Remove from the tin and allow to cool on a wire rack.
4. To make the frosting, blend all the ingredients (except the banana chips) until smooth.
5. Ice the cooled cake and decorate with banana chips.

Glazed ginger loaf

250 g butter, softened
1 cup sugar
2½ Tbsp golden syrup
4 tsp ground ginger
1 tsp mixed spice
a pinch of salt
3 jumbo eggs, at room temperature, separated
2 cups cake flour, sifted
¾ cup milk
1 tsp bicarbonate of soda
2½ Tbsp cold water

GLAZE

1½ cups icing sugar, sifted
¼ cup water
½ tsp ground ginger, sifted

1. Preheat the oven to 180 °C and grease and flour a 35 x 11 cm loaf tin.
2. Cream the butter and sugar. Add the syrup, ginger, mixed spice, salt and egg yolks.
3. Add the flour alternately with the milk.
4. Dissolve the bicarbonate of soda in the water and add to the mixture.
5. Beat the egg whites until stiff and fold into the mixture.
6. Pour into the loaf tin and bake for 50–60 minutes. When cool, remove from the tin.
7. To make the glaze, mix together all the ingredients.
8. To make it a pouring consistency, you may need to add extra water.
9. Pour over the cooled cake.

Blitz torte

110 g butter, softened
1¼ cups sugar + extra for sprinkling
1 cup cake flour
1 tsp baking powder
a pinch of salt
4 eggs, separated
½ tsp vanilla essence
3 Tbsp milk
½ tsp ground cinnamon
1 cup flaked almonds, toasted
1 cup fresh cream, whipped
¼ cup cherries (optional)

1. Preheat the oven to 180 °C and grease two 20 cm-diameter baking tins.
2. Cream the butter and ½ cup sugar until the mixture appears white.
3. In a separate bowl, sift together the flour, baking powder and salt.
4. Beat the egg yolks, adding the vanilla essence and milk.
5. Slowly add the egg mixture and the dry ingredients to the creamed butter mixture and blend well.
6. Divide this mixture between the baking tins.
7. In another bowl, beat the egg whites until stiff, gradually adding ¾ cup sugar.
8. Spread this meringue over the unbaked mixtures.
9. Sprinkle with a little extra sugar, as well as the cinnamon and ½ cup flaked almonds.
10. Bake for 30 minutes. Remove from the tins when cool.
11. Place the first cake, meringue-side down, and spread with the whipped cream.
12. Scatter over the cherries (if using) and the remaining flaked almonds. Place the second cake on top, meringue-side up.
13. Chill in the fridge for 30 minutes before serving.

Cheesy scones

1 cup cake flour
1 dessertspoon baking powder
1 tsp salt
1 tsp mustard powder
1 cup grated Cheddar cheese
1 cup milk
a few drops of Tabasco® sauce

1. Preheat the oven to 190 °C and grease two mini-muffin tins.
2. Sift the flour, baking powder, salt and mustard powder in a bowl. Stir in the cheese.
3. Add the milk and Tabasco® sauce, and mix well.
4. Spoon into the muffin tins and bake for 15 minutes. These are perfect served with either tea or tomato soup, or eaten straight out of the tin. For an interesting flavour sensation, serve with anchovy butter (see page 75).

Makes 24

Coconut macaroon cake

This cake has two layers that are baked in the same tin.

BOTTOM LAYER

175 g butter, softened

¾ cup sugar

1½ cups cake flour

1½ tsp baking powder

a pinch of salt

4 egg yolks (keep the egg whites for the top layer)

½ tsp vanilla essence

½ cup milk

TOP LAYER

4 egg whites

¾ cup sugar

2¼ cups desiccated coconut

1. Preheat the oven to 180 °C and grease and flour a chiffon or 23 cm tube tin.
2. For the bottom layer, cream the butter and sugar.
3. In a separate bowl, sift together the flour, baking powder and salt.
4. Fold the dry ingredients into the butter mixture. Add the egg yolks, vanilla essence and milk alternately.
5. Spread the mixture in the bottom of the chiffon tin.
6. For the top layer, beat the egg whites until stiff and gradually add the sugar. Add the coconut, mixing by hand. Spread this over the bottom layer of the cake.
7. Bake for 5 minutes, then reduce the temperature to 160 °C and bake for a further 45 minutes, until the coconut is crisp. This is delicious served with a berry coulis (see page 61).

Lollipop tarts

2 sheets puff pastry
12 thick wooden kebab sticks
 or ice-cream sticks
1 egg, lightly beaten

1. Roll out the pastry to 10 mm thick.
   Using a 6 cm cutter, cut 24 rounds.
2. Preheat the oven to 180 °C and grease
   a baking tray.
3. Prepare your chosen filling (see below
   and opposite for filling options).
4. Taking 12 pastry rounds, place 1 Tbsp
   filling in the middle of each. Place a
   stick in the centre, about a third below
   the top of the round, and cover each
   with a second pastry round. Gently
   press the edges of the rounds together
   with a fork to seal. Place on the
   baking tray and brush with the egg.
5. Bake until golden, 10–15 minutes.
   Allow the lollipops to cool on the tray
   before picking them up.

Makes 12

Sweet strawberry and apple
180 g tinned pie apple slices, chopped
5 large strawberries, hulled and sliced
3 Tbsp grape jam/preserve

1. Mix all the ingredients together.

Peanut butter and banana
3 medium bananas, roughly mashed
¼ cup chunky peanut butter
2 Tbsp caramel treat

1. Mix all the ingredients together.

Salmon and mushroom

500 g mushrooms, sliced
1 red pepper, deseeded and
    finely chopped
olive oil for sautéing
1 Tbsp cake flour
1 cup milk
freshly ground black pepper to taste
½ tsp paprika
½ tsp fresh lemon juice
¼ cup grated mozzarella cheese
350 g tinned salmon, deboned
    and flaked

1. Sauté the mushrooms and red
    pepper in a saucepan in olive oil.
    Sprinkle over the flour and slowly
    add the milk. Season with the pepper,
    paprika and lemon juice.
2. Add the cheese and mix well.
    Add the salmon, stirring until
    combined. Adjust seasoning and
    remove from the heat.

Spinach surprise

200 g spinach
olive oil for braising
a drop of fresh lemon juice
a pinch of ground nutmeg
125 g smooth cream cheese
100 g Cheddar cheese, grated
1 Tbsp chopped fresh parsley
sea salt and freshly ground
    black pepper to taste

1. In a frying pan, braise the spinach in
    olive oil with lemon juice until soft.
    Remove and squeeze out all
    the water.
2. Place the spinach in a bowl and add
    the nutmeg, cream cheese, Cheddar
    cheese and parsley. Season to taste.
3. Whizz in a blender for a few seconds.

TREAT

Pronounced [treet]

(Verb tr.) To act or behave in a specified manner toward someone; to deal with or represent artistically in a specified manner or style; to provide with food, entertainment or gifts at one's own expense; to give (someone or oneself) something pleasurable, for example a *chocolate slice*. **(Verb intr.)** A source of glorious glee or pleasure. **(Noun)** A sweet tooth's delight; containing decadent swirls of sugariness; an extra helping of indulgence; no holds barred; eat the last crumb sort-of-recipes. *Heaven*.

Greek biscuit twist
with pistachios and green glacé cherries

250 g butter, melted
2 cups cake flour
½ cup icing sugar
1 tsp vanilla essence
¾ cup roughly chopped
   pistachios, toasted
½ cup chopped green glacé cherries
extra icing sugar for coating

1. Preheat the oven to 180 °C and
   grease a baking tray.
2. Melt the butter in a saucepan.
3. Add the flour, icing sugar and
   vanilla essence, and mix well. Add
   the pistachios and cherries, and mix.
4. Roll the dough into small balls or
   roll it out and use cookie cutters to
   create shapes.
5. Place on the greased baking tray
   and gently press the biscuits with
   the back of a fork.
6. Bake for 10–12 minutes. Allow to cool
   before tossing in icing sugar to coat.

Ginger rounds

150 g butter, softened
¼ cup brown sugar
1½ cups cake flour, sifted
1 tsp baking powder
1¼ tsp ground ginger
175 g crystallised ginger in syrup, finely
 diced + extra for decorating

1. Preheat the oven to 180 °C.
 Grease a 30 x 24 cm baking tin.
2. Melt the butter in a saucepan.
 Remove from the heat
 and stir in the sugar.
3. Add the flour, baking powder
 and ground ginger, and mix well. Stir
 in the ginger pieces with the syrup.
4. Pour the mixture into the greased
 tin and bake for approximately
 20 minutes until golden brown.
5. Remove from the oven and allow
 to cool for 10 minutes before
 cutting into squares or rounds
 using a scalloped cookie cutter.
6. Decorate with extra bits of
 crystallised ginger.

Makes approximately 18

Striped fudge caramel strip

BASE

250 g butter, softened

½ cup castor sugar

2¼ cups cake flour, sifted

½ cup cornflour

a pinch of salt

CARAMEL CENTRE

125 g butter, softened

¾ cup treacle sugar

2 Tbsp golden syrup

1 x 385 g tin condensed milk

½ tsp vanilla essence

TOPPING

200 g Albany chocolate

70 g butter, softened

1 tsp vanilla essence

3 x 100 g Peppermint Crisp bars, crushed (optional)

1. Preheat the oven to 150 °C. Grease a 25–35 cm square baking tin.
2. To make the base, cream the butter and castor sugar until pale in colour. Add the remaining base ingredients and mix well.
3. Press the mixture into the tin and bake for 15–20 minutes. Allow to cool.
4. To make the caramel centre, heat the butter, treacle sugar, syrup and condensed milk in a saucepan over a low heat. Stir continuously for 7–10 minutes until the mixture boils. Remove from the heat, add the vanilla essence and mix.
5. Allow to cool before pouring over the cooled base. Place in the fridge to set.
6. To make the topping, melt the Albany chocolate, butter and vanilla essence in a double boiler and mix well.
7. Pour over the set caramel centre and allow to cool slightly. If using, sprinkle the crushed Peppermint Crisp over the top and return to the fridge to set.
8. Cut into squares or long strips.

Makes approximately 20

Crispy, golden chocolate squares

125 g butter
1½ Tbsp golden syrup
3 x 100 g Bar One® or Mars® bar
   chocolate bars
4 cups Rice Krispies®
2 x 200 g milk chocolate slabs
crushed Cadbury Flake®, Crunchie®,
   Whispers® or any delicious chocolate
   you prefer (optional)

1. Grease a 32 x 23 cm baking tray.
2. Melt the butter, syrup and caramel chocolates in a saucepan over a low heat.
3. Remove from the heat and add the Rice Krispies®. Mix until combined and pour onto the greased tray.
4. Place in the fridge to set.
5. Once the base is set, melt the milk chocolate in a double boiler.
6. Pour over the base and allow to cool.
7. When cool, sprinkle over the crushed chocolate (if using) and return to the fridge to set.
8. When set, remove from the fridge and allow to return to room temperature before cutting into squares. Store in the fridge.

Makes approximately 20 squares

Chocolate slices

200 g Albany chocolate
100 g butter
¼ cup fresh cream
¼ cup golden syrup
1 x 200 g pkt Marie or tea
    biscuits, crushed
1 x 200 g pkt digestive biscuits, crushed
1 Tbsp Kahlua

TOPPING
300 g good-quality milk chocolate
50 g digestive biscuits, crushed
50 g flaked almonds, toasted (optional)

1. Grease a 35 x 24 cm baking tin.
2. Melt the Albany chocolate, butter,
    cream and syrup in a double boiler
    over a medium heat. Stir well until
    the chocolate has melted. Remove
    from the heat and allow the mixture
    to cool slightly.
3. Toss the crushed biscuits with the
    Kahlua in a bowl.
4. Pour the melted chocolate mixture
    over the biscuits and mix well.
5. Pour the mixture into the greased
    tin, smoothing it over. Place in
    the fridge to set.
6. When set, melt the milk chocolate
    for the topping in a double boiler
    until smooth and pour over the
    set mixture.
7. Top with the digestive biscuits and
    almonds (if using), and return to the
    fridge. Allow to set until hard, before
    slicing into fingers or cutting into
    shapes using cookie cutters.

Makes approximately 18

Lemon slices

CRUST

250 g unsalted butter, at room temperature

½ cup sugar

2 cups cake flour, sifted

a pinch of salt

FILLING

6 extra-large eggs, at room temperature

3 cups sugar

2 Tbsp lemon zest

200 ml fresh lemon juice

1 cup cake flour

icing sugar for dusting

1. To make the crust, cream the butter and sugar until pale using an electric mixer.
2. In a separate bowl, combine the flour and salt. With the mixer on a low speed, add the flour to the butter until just combined.
3. Turn out the dough onto a floured board and form a ball. Flatten with floured hands and press into a springform tin (28 x 18 cm), building up a 3 cm edge. Chill in the fridge.
4. Preheat the oven to 180 °C and bake the crust for 15 minutes until lightly browned. Leaving the oven on, allow to cool while you make the filling.
5. Whisk the eggs, sugar, zest, juice and flour. Pour over the cooled crust and bake for 30–35 minutes until set. Remove and cool at room temperature.
6. Chill before cutting into fingers, and dust with icing sugar. The filling is gooey so keep the slices cool until serving.

Makes 20–30 fingers

Milk tart

125 g butter, melted
1 x 200 g pkt Marie or
    tea biscuits, crushed
1 x 385 g tin condensed milk
4 cups milk
1 egg
3 Tbsp cornflour
3 Tbsp custard powder
¼ cup sugar
ground cinnamon for decorating

1. Spray a rectangular ovenproof dish
   (approximately 28 cm long) with
   non-stick cooking spray.
2. Mix the butter and crushed biscuits,
   and press into the dish.
3. In the microwave, heat the condensed
   milk and milk for 7–10 minutes
   until almost boiling.
4. In a separate bowl, mix the egg,
   cornflour, custard powder and sugar
   to form a paste. If lumpy, allow it
   to stand for a while.
5. Add the custard mixture to the
   heated milk and stir. Microwave for
   approximately 10 minutes to thicken,
   checking every 3–5 minutes and
   whisking each time.
6. Pour the mixture over the biscuit
   base while hot. Sift over some ground
   cinnamon and place in the fridge
   overnight to set.

Nut brittle

150 g sugar
100 g raw almonds, roughly chopped
50 g pistachios, roughly chopped
   or 50 g peanuts, left whole
50 g raw cashews, roughly chopped

1. Line a baking tray with greaseproof
    paper.
2. Dissolve the sugar in a saucepan
    over a medium heat. As it begins
    to boil, shake the pan. Cook until
    golden and pour onto the lined
    baking tray.
3. Scatter over the almonds, pistachios
    and cashews, pressing them into
    the caramel.
4. Allow to cool and set before
    breaking the brittle into shards.

Pronounced [sip]

(Verb) Drink – a liquid – a little at a time; take small tastes of; sip something, especially repeatedly, like a *fizzy flavoured float fortified with condensed milk*; absorb (slowly) *gin with a lime-herb extract*. **(Noun)** An instance of sipping; a small taste of a liquid or a lingering slurp of *thick ice cream wafer chocolate blend*. **(Verb tr.)** To sip and savour the tang of *pineapple sake*; to soak up *litchi granita*; to absorb the *freshest fruit sap*. **Indemnity:** Slurping; glugging; gulping; swigging; spooning; stirring; sipping at your own risk.

SIP

Watermelon, raspberry and rosewater cocktail

120 g raspberries
¼ watermelon, deseeded and chopped
1 Tbsp rosewater
1 measure simple syrup (see below)
a slice of watermelon and rose petals for garnishing

1. Purée all the ingredients in a blender and serve over crushed ice, garnished with a slice of watermelon and rose petals.

Serves 4–6

Simple syrup recipe
for cocktails

1 cup water
½ cup white sugar

1. Place the ingredients in a saucepan and bring to the boil.
2. Reduce the heat and simmer for 5 minutes.
3. Pour into a container and allow to cool before using.

Kiwi, mint and lime crush

4 kiwi fruits, peeled and diced
4–6 sprigs mint, washed
zest and juice of 1 lime
1 measure simple syrup (see page 364) or 1½ cups clear apple juice

1. Purée all the ingredients in a blender, pour into a container
   and freeze for 20 minutes.
2. Remove from the freezer and break up the ice crystals.
   Refreeze for approximately 1 hour.

Serves 4–6

Gin
with lime–herb extract

1 cup finely chopped fresh mint
1 cup finely chopped fresh basil
1 lime, cut into quarters
zest and juice of 1 lime
3 cups gin
a pinch of sea salt
¼ cup sugar
crushed ice for serving

1. Crush the mint and basil in a pestle and mortar.
2. Place the herbs, lime quarters and lime zest in a jug.
3. Add the gin, lime juice and salt, and stir in the sugar. Cover and refrigerate overnight.
4. Remove the lime wedges and zest before serving and pour into shot glasses with crushed ice.

Serves 8–10

Cucumber and peach martini

1 x small English cucumber, sliced lengthways using a peeler
3 peaches, peeled and cut into 3 mm-thick wedges
1 bottle vodka
1 bottle vermouth
3 guavas, peeled and thinly sliced (optional)

1. Place two strips of curled cucumber and two peach slices in each martini glass.
2. Liquidise the remaining cucumber and press through a sieve to strain.
3. Make a standard vodka martini: for each glass mix ¼ cup vodka and 1 Tbsp vermouth with ice cubes. Stir well and strain the ice cubes.
4. Mix the vodka martini with the cucumber juice and pour over the cucumber and peaches in the martini glasses.
5. Decorate each with a sliver of guava if desired.

Serves 6–8

Litchi granita

1 litre litchi juice
½ cup chopped fresh purple basil
1 bottle vodka

1. Pour the litchi juice into a shallow dish and freeze.
   Remove from the freezer, scrape with a fork
   to create crushed litchi ice and refreeze.
2. Repeat this process twice more, but instead of
   refreezing a third time, scoop the crushed litchi ice
   into a blender and whizz with the chopped basil.
3. Scoop the granita into small glasses
   and cover each with a tot of vodka.

Serves 6–8

Frozen berry iced tea

1 litre good-quality black tea
2 cups assorted fresh berries frozen in ice trays, or frozen berries scooped
   into ice trays and refrozen
chopped fresh mint for garnishing

1. Allow the tea to cool in a large jug.
2. Fill with frozen berry ice cubes and garnish with fresh mint.

Serves 4–6

Pineapple sake (or vodka)

1 x 750 ml bottle sake or vodka
1 x 300 g tin pineapple chunks in syrup

1. Place the alcohol and pineapple (with the syrup) in a jug.
2. Cover and chill in the fridge overnight.

Serves 8–10

Fresh juice bar

Place an assortment of fresh fruit, cut into chunks, in large glass containers. Blend fresh juices for guests, or allow them to blend juices for themselves.

King Cone milkshakes

6 x King Cones®, softened
6 x wafer biscuits

1. Blend the ice creams in a blender and pour into glasses.
2. Decorate with the wafer biscuits.

Serves 4–6

Iced coffee float

1 litre good-quality coffee ice cream
1 x 385 g tin condensed milk
2 Tbsp finely crushed coffee granules
1 litre strong good-quality coffee,
  cooled with ice cubes

1. Scoop the ice cream into balls and roll
   in the condensed milk and crushed coffee.
   Place on a baking tray and refreeze.
2. Place the frozen balls in glasses and
   cover with the cooled coffee.

Serves 4–6

Condensed milk-infused fizzy floats

1 litre good-quality vanilla ice cream
1 x 385 g tin condensed milk
1 litre Coca-Cola®/Creme Soda/Fanta Grape®/Sparberry®

1. Scoop the vanilla ice cream into balls. Place on a baking tray and freeze.
2. When well frozen, remove from the tray and roll in the condensed milk. Refreeze on the baking tray.
3. Pour your choice of soda in a glass and add a ball of ice cream.

Tip: For a strawberry-flavoured float, use strawberry ice cream and raspberry soda.

Serves 4–6

RECIPE INDEX

Pronounced [res-*uh*-pee] [in-deks] (Noun) Something that serves to guide, point out or otherwise facilitate reference, especially: an alphabetised list of names and *recipes* treated in a printed work, giving the page or pages on which each item is mentioned; *an alphabetical gastronomic guide.*

Oven temperatures

Celsius (C)	Fahrenheit (F)	Gas mark
100 °C	200 °F	¼
110 °C	225 °F	¼
120 °C	250 °F	½
140 °C	275 °F	1
150 °C	300 °F	2
160 °C	325 °F	3
180 °C	350 °F	4
190 °C	375 °F	5
200 °C	400 °F	6
220 °C	425 °F	7
230 °C	450 °F	8
240 °C	475 °F	9

Conversion table

Metric	US cups	Imperial
5 ml	1 tsp	1 tsp
15 ml	1 Tbsp	1 Tbsp
60 ml	4 Tbsp (¼ cup)	2 fl oz
80 ml	⅓ cup	2¾ fl oz
125 ml	½ cup	4½ fl oz
160 ml	⅔ cup	5½ fl oz
200 ml	¾ cup	7 fl oz
250 ml	1 cup	9 fl oz

Thanks

Pronounced [thangks]
(Noun, plural) An expression of gratitude; an acknowledgment of appreciation;
a statement acknowledging something or someone ... *our families; our friends;
our supportive publishing team at Struik – Linda, Bev and Bronwen; and our fabulous
photographer Vanessa Lewis and fashionable food stylist Taryne Jakobi ...
for enabling us to create something truly worth* **savouring**.

Cover and inside cover props from Eclectic Gifts, thanks to Linda and Stephanie.
A special thank you to Michael Lewis for his valuable input and expert eye,
and to Jeremy Carlsson and Richard Sutton, and the conceptspark team.

Published in 2011 by Struik Lifestyle
(an imprint of Random House Struik (Pty) Ltd)
Company Reg. No. 1966/003153/07
80 McKenzie Street, Cape Town 8001
PO Box 1144, Cape Town, 8000, South Africa

www.randomstruik.co.za

ISBN 978-1-77007-827-7

Publisher: Linda de Villiers
Managing editor: Cecilia Barfield
Editor: Bronwen Leak
Designer: Beverley Dodd
Photographer: Vanessa Lewis (www.ninasaycheese.com)
Food and décor stylist: Taryne Jakobi (www.tarynejakobi.co.za)
Proofreader and indexer: Joy Clack

Reproduction: Hirt & Carter Cape (Pty) Ltd
Printing and binding: Tien Wah Press (Pte) Limited, Singapore